Teaching the Restless

Teaching the Restless

One School's Remarkable
No-Ritalin Approach to
Helping Children
Learn and Succeed

Chris Mercogliano

Beacon Press, Boston

BEACON PRESS
25 Beacon Street
Boston, Massachusetts 02108-2892
www.beacon.org

Beacon Press books
are published under the auspices of
the Unitarian Universalist Association of Congregations.

07 06 05 04 03   8 7 6 5 4 3 2 1

This book is printed on acid-free paper that meets the
uncoated paper ANSI/NISO specifications for permanence as revised in 1992.

Text Design by Isaac Tobin

LIBRARY OF CONGRESS CATALOGING-IN-PUBLICATION DATA

Mercogliano, Chris.
Teaching the restless : one school's remarkable no-Ritalin approach to
helping children learn and succeed / Chris Mercogliano.
    p. cm.
Includes bibliographical references and index.
  ISBN 0-8070-3246-8 (cloth : alk. paper)
  1. Hyperactive children—Education—United States. I. Title.
  LC4712.M47 2003
  371.93—dc21
                                         2003014847

To Sophia

Introduction

This book is a response to the troubling increase in the number of children being prescribed biopsychiatric medications because they don't fit into America's classrooms. Though there are virtually no comprehensive statistics, it is estimated that anywhere from 15 to 20 percent of American boys are currently taking methylphenidate, more commonly known as Ritalin, or other stimulant drugs to control their behavior in school.[1] The majority begin taking these drugs at age six or seven, but the minimum age is creeping lower all the time. According to a study published in the February 2000 issue of the *Journal of the American Medical Association,* the number of Ritalin prescriptions written for two- to four-year-olds went up nearly 300 percent between 1991 and 1995.[2]

Biopsychiatric medications like Ritalin are the medical establishment's response to a loose collection of behaviors in children that are seen as evidence of organic disorders. Today, the labels for these disorders have proliferated almost to the point of absurdity. Persistently disobedient kids are now said to suffer from conduct disorder (CD); or, if they are really tough cases, oppositional defiance disorder (ODD). Youngsters who don't get along with others have antisocial personality disorder (APD). For nervous, flighty children it's generalized anxiety disorder (GAD), and if they habitually repeat unusual or dysfunctional behaviors, then it's obsessive compulsive disorder

(OCD). For our purposes in this book, I will refer only to the label that is the current catchall for the majority of pupils who are the flies in the classroom ointment: attention deficit hyperactivity disorder, otherwise known as ADHD.

ADHD has ignited a whole host of conflicting reactions. At one end of the spectrum is a large group of mainstream educators, child psychologists, pediatricians, neuroscientists, and parents who absolutely believe in the existence of ADHD. To them, children whom they judge to be too active, too distractible, too willful, too impulsive, too impatient, too emotional, or too aggressive are suffering from a chemical imbalance in the brain, supposedly genetic in origin. The imbalance results in a shortage of the neurotransmitters that enable the brain to regulate its own activities, such as paying attention and controlling impulses. Stimulant drugs supposedly "wake up" the control center responsible for sending out those neurotransmitters, thus rendering the child more manageable and able to focus.

At the other end of the spectrum is a smaller though rapidly expanding coalition of concerned psychologists, scientists, and parents who are convinced that there is no such thing as ADHD. They decry the absence of scientific evidence of the disorder and view the use of drugs as an unwarranted and harmful intervention.

In between these two camps lies a wide assortment of groups and individuals with differing positions. For example, some believe in the validity of ADHD but feel that the drugs used to treat it are risky and overprescribed. They advocate behavioral forms of intervention or other alternative treatments such as special diets, homeopathy, or herbal remedies. Others utilize biofeedback to improve the ability of distractible, impulsive children to concentrate and control their own actions. Still others assert that ADHD kids are mentally gifted and need special learning environments to match their exceptional conceptual powers and high-speed minds.

The controversy over ADHD is a reflection of the issue's complexity. Many of the children in this country labeled with ADHD have nothing wrong with them at all. The trouble lies in school environments that fail to support their unique needs and natures. Other labeled children exhibit early learning difficulties that are not organic in origin but are caused by forcing academics on them before they are ready, willing, and able to invest themselves in the learning process. Still others have real problems coping with life both in and outside school. However, it is my belief that they are *not* suffering from an organic disorder. Rather, their dysfunctional and antisocial behaviors are distress signals: symptomatic expressions of unmet needs and emotional turbulence—not disease.

To date, the majority of books about ADHD have been written by pediatricians and psychologists. I approach the subject from another vantage point, that of a teacher with thirty years' worth of highly instructive experience in a privately funded, freedom-based inner-city educational alternative for children ages two through fourteen in Albany, New York, known as the Free School.

The school's independent status permits us to experiment with different educational strategies as we see fit. This means we are a veritable laboratory for developing ways to help children who don't conform to conventional academic and behavioral norms to relax, focus, modulate emotional expression, make responsible choices, appreciate themselves and others, and forge lasting friendships—all key prerequisites for learning—without assigning them medical labels and without resorting to the use of biopsychiatric drugs.

Approximately half of our fifty students come to us after experiencing serious academic and/or behavioral problems in their previous schools. Many of their parents seek us out because they've become concerned over the negative effects labeling and drugging have on their kids and have heard that we maintain a strict policy against labeling or drugging even the most trying child. The other half of our students are happy, easygoing natural learners who would probably thrive just about anywhere. They come to us because their parents want them in an environment where they will have plenty of physical, intellectual, and emotional freedom, where they will be nurtured and loved, and where their individuality will be respected at all times.

The Free School's success with children who for whatever reason don't fit into conventional school settings can be traced to a set of four core principles.

1. Every child has his or her own unique developmental trajectory. It is of little importance to us at the Free School whether a student learns to read by the age of three or the age of ten, because we know that different children are ready to learn different things at different times.

2. A school must be a community—the real, not the euphemistic, kind—where the children have a say in its governance and are encouraged to work out their differences among themselves whenever possible. True communities are inclusive by nature and entrust all of their members with responsibility for the well-being of the whole. Cooperation is valued over competition, and no one is left behind.

3. A child's emotional health is of paramount importance in school. Happy children are ready learners and are intrinsically sociable. Or as Joseph Chilton Pearce, author of *The Magical Child* and *Evolution's End* so aptly puts it, "The head will follow the heart every time."[3]

4. All children need to be loved and touched, especially children who are struggling to establish their footing in the world. They need validation and permission to be themselves, not carrot-and-stick prodding. They need warm special attention, not cold special classifications.

To illustrate the above principles, I followed a handful of students through a year at the Free School. The six boys—William, Damian, Carl, Brian, Walter, and Mark—and three girls—Mumasatou, Tanya, and Gabrielle—all were either labeled and drugged in their previous schools or would have been had they not thrown in their lot with us. While in my mind there is no such thing as a "typical" child, these nine represent the millions of children across the country—estimates currently run as high as 6 million—who have been diagnosed with learning and behavioral disorders and prescribed corresponding biopsychiatric medications. I have made every effort to make each child's story vivid and intimate, because all too often educational theory and practice are based on an analysis that applies only to hypothetical, not real, children. In addition, I interrupt their narratives from time to time to examine certain relevant scientific studies. These, I hope, will help readers better understand the psychological and sociological roots of childhood distress.

This book will not present any mass-producible solutions or any templates for school reform. Instead, it will suggest a shift in how we as a society perceive children who learn and behave in problematic ways, away from the mechanical theory of an epidemic of faulty brain chemistry and toward a compassionate consideration of the individual quality of their lives, both inner and outer. It is my profound hope that by zooming in on a handful of challenging kids I can model for parents, teachers, administrators, and policy makers alike how it is possible without labels and drugs to help distressed children grow into authentic, competent individuals eager to make the most of their lives and contribute to the world around them.

My ongoing work with young people has convinced me that extraordinary things can happen when kids work and play together within a community that tolerates personal differences and idiosyncratic behavior, takes developmental timetables with a grain of salt, refuses to turn learning into a mandatory chore, relies on trust and personal responsibility instead of compulsion and coercion, and respects a child's inalienable right to say "no."

I hope the following stories convince some of you, too.

Teaching the Restless

1

William's mother, Irene, telephoned me in early August. She was referred to us by her community-based health clinic, where she brought her son to be examined after he had fitfully completed kindergarten in his neighborhood parochial school. William had been displaying all of the classic signs of so-called attention deficit hyperactivity disorder, or ADHD. In school he had been inattentive, restless, impulsive, disruptive, at times combative. He frequently refused to do as he was told, and as a result, his parents were called in for numerous conferences with the teacher. When the situation only continued to deteriorate, Irene and her husband were urged by the principal to have William "evaluated," and please not to bring him back for first grade.

The health-care worker who made the referral had heard of our reputation for success with children I shall hereafter refer to—with tongue in cheek—as "Ritalin kids." She suggested to William's parents that they give the Free School a try as an alternative to putting William on medication and enrolling him in another conventional school setting.

William's nine-year-old brother, meanwhile, had been taking Ritalin since he was five. The boys' parents, an intact, articulate, African-American couple in their mid-thirties, were not at all happy about its effect on him, so they decided to try a different approach with William.

I spoke at length with Irene, as I always do with prospective parents, in order to describe our unorthodox approach to education in general and to dealing with children with learning and behavioral problems in particular. I began by explaining to her that there are no compulsory lessons or classes. This prompted a very common response to such a radical statement: "What if my son just decides to play all day?"

"One of society's most closely guarded secrets is how much children learn while they are playing," came my first-level response. "Not just physical and social skills, but important cognitive ones, too."

Her silence indicated I wasn't getting through, so I added, "A great deal of language development occurs through play, and play also develops the imagination, which, as Albert Einstein once said, is much more important than knowledge."

Still no response. Finally, I suggested that William must be one of those highly intelligent kids who do their learning on the run for a while, kind of like the stereotypical businessman rushing off to work still tying his necktie, with an unread newspaper under his arm and a piece of hastily buttered toast clenched between his teeth.

"William is very smart. He just doesn't seem to want to apply himself," said Irene, her voice a mixture of frustration and concern.

"Remember that he's only six," I replied. "He may not be ready to settle down and focus on sequential tasks like reading and math. You know, schools are putting more and more pressure on kids at younger and younger ages, and it's not a good thing. Especially for boys like William."

The conversation turned to behavioral issues. "I just don't want William to go through what he went through last year; that was terrible," Irene reflected. "I know he misbehaved a lot, but he's not a bad kid."

I was relieved to hear that Irene was both acknowledging her son's difficulties and yet still on his side.

"It sounds as though a lot of what he did last year was trying to resist an environment that was too rigid and controlling," I returned. "Which is not to say he won't have problems here too, but when he does we will deal with them differently."

I went on to explain that, aside from having to adhere to a few non-negotiable rules with regard to health, safety, and respect, William would be free to set his own agenda in school. To the extent that he was trustworthy, he would have the run of the building. At the same time, I assured her, we would set firm and appropriate limits on his behavior as each situation called for them.

Then I asked her not to expect miracles overnight. Although, thankfully, William had spent only a single year trapped in a classroom where he was viewed as a problem and a failure, likely as not he had already internalized a negative image of himself and learned an array of dysfunctional behaviors that would take him time to unlearn.

I could tell Irene wasn't entirely convinced, but it seemed to me we had at least established a rapport on which we could build as the year progressed.

Observing William enter with his mother on the first day of school, I am treated to a fly-on-the-wall view of one of the primary patterns I see underlying the formation of the so-called ADHD child. With William firmly by the arm, Irene gently but insistently pulls him over to the table where breakfast is being served and where Nancy, who codirects the school with me, and I are talking over morning coffee. Mother and son are so engrossed in their private dance that they appear not to notice we are watching.

"Good morning, Irene," I say as I get up and extend my hand in greeting. "It's wonderful to finally meet you." Then, to the boy clinging sheepishly to her coat, "And you must be William. It's nice to meet you, too."

"Would you like some breakfast, William?" Nancy asks. "We've got scrambled eggs, and toast with cream cheese and jelly."

A handsome, sweet-looking boy quite tall for his age, William doesn't answer. He is too busy leaning against his mother's legs and studying the patterns on his new leather basketball shoes. Irene looks down at him and repeats the question several times before he finally mumbles softly that he isn't hungry.

Irene is an attractive woman with a broad, open face always hinting at a smile. She is clearly pregnant. It is difficult to engage her in conversation because her attention remains on the boy still nervously attached to her side. When she tries to get him to part with his jacket, she meets with no more success than she had in getting him to eat. I notice William gradually becoming aware of the kids playing on the large wooden jungle gym at the opposite end of the "big room," as we call the high-ceilinged forty-by-forty-foot space in the upstairs of our building where the preschool is housed and where we all eat breakfast and lunch together, family-style. Just as I was hoping, the moment soon arrives when he releases his grip on his mother and zooms over to jump and climb with the other kids. Now Irene and I can continue our earlier conversation.

While we watch William scale the jungle gym with the agility of a young cougar, I explain to Irene that kids like hers with a large amount of energy and acumen need ample opportunity to be physical. That's why we have the indoor climbing structure, with a double layer of queen-size mattresses underneath the horizontal ladder section for safety, and an even bigger structure in the backyard.

"You know, most of William's so-called hyperactivity will

disappear almost immediately here because he can be as active as he needs to be," I say. "Downstairs we have a big mat for tumbling and wrestling, and also a punching bag, and then there is a woodshop and an art room that he can work in whenever he asks."

"What about his reading?" she asks anxiously. "I think I told you on the phone he isn't reading yet."

"Nancy has a reading class every morning for her first graders that William can attend if he wants to. Or he can work with her one on one, if he prefers," I explain.

Irene nods uncertainly, and so I continue talking. "It's not that we've made freedom a religion. It's just we've discovered over the years that kids learn faster and more easily when the motivation comes from inside them. And they behave better when they are expected to be responsible for themselves and each other."

"I just want my son to do the things I know he's capable of doing."

"I have no doubt that at some point William will make up his mind that he wants to learn to read. And when he does, it won't be any big deal because he's so smart. The best part about not forcing children to read prematurely is that when they do learn, they enjoy the process and it doesn't leave a bad taste in their mouths."

It is clear that I am stretching Irene's ability to suspend her disbelief. It doesn't help when I add, "Given William's negative experience in kindergarten, and his high energy level, don't be surprised if it takes a while before he decides to join in on academic activities."

My honesty is hardly reassuring. But I never want to leave parents with false expectations, especially about an issue as highly charged as reading. This is why we always have children visit the school on a trial basis for at least a week, so that all involved know what they are getting themselves into before they make any long-term commitments.

Irene glances at her watch and announces that it is time for her to leave. She thanks me for my time and then calls across the room to William, who is so engrossed in climbing and jumping that he scarcely acknowledges his mother's good-bye. He finally waves distractedly to her just as she is disappearing through the door.

William spends his first day like a kitten in an unfamiliar place. Almost constantly in motion, he explores the nooks and crannies of every room in the school, stopping briefly to eat a sizable meal at lunchtime. Amid his travels he begins to establish his personal curriculum. For instance, he infuriates just about everyone with whom he comes into contact, thanks to his pushy, entitled way of relating to others. His sense of boundaries is still quite immature. Just like a toddler, he assumes that every interesting object within reach is fair game for him to grab and investigate. His location in the building can easily be tracked by the cries of "Hey, that's mine! GIVE IT BACK!" or "Please be quiet; we're trying to read a story in here!"

William makes no bones about his disregard for limits. But as is usually the case with newcomers, the school community tries to make allowances for his naiveté. With a certain stretched tolerance, everyone lets him down easy with first and second warnings. Thus, William's maiden voyage on the good ship Free School ends without serious incident. At three o'clock, Nancy gives Irene an honest report, telling her that the honeymoon is likely to end sooner rather than later due to William's proclivity for running afoul of the other kids, particularly those younger and smaller than himself.

The next morning my wife suggests I bring my eldest daughter's dog to school with me. A gentle, high-energy eternal puppy, Lakota is a perfect match for kids like William. The two of them spend the first hour roaming the building and backyard playground together. The dog is infinitely more tolerant of William's rough edges, and this gives him a little breathing room as he begins to try to find his place in an environment so full of activity that a great many first-time visitors perceive it as nothing short of chaos.

Although William is technically in Nancy's first grade class, I suspect he will choose to spend a lot of time with me and my group of second and third graders, most of whom happen to be boys this year. It is already obvious that he is much more drawn to me simply because I am a man. Also, his athleticism is likely to match him up with my boys, to whom he is already equal in both size and determination. We arrange class groupings loosely for just this reason, so that we can meet children's needs as they present themselves and avoid unnecessary conflict and frustration. Nancy, even with all of her acquired savvy in handling rambunctious, willful boys (she has been at the school almost as long as I have and has a highly energetic eight-year-old son of her own), would expect to have no more luck with him than William's teacher did last year if she too were confined in a classroom with William for six hours a day.

It isn't until after lunch that William makes his first serious mistake, when he refuses to do his share of cleaning up the lunchroom tables and floor. The elementary-age kids are organized into five daily crews, with an older student serving as crew chief. Although participation in this necessary chore is not optional—the school has no custodial staff—the kids generally carry out the cleaning willingly and well.

"I don't like cleaning and you can't make me!" William proclaims defiantly to Janine, his unlucky boss.

This proud young warrior isn't about to take orders from any girl. But little does he know that Janine is a no-nonsense twelve-year-old who has had plenty of practice dealing with recalcitrant younger siblings at home.

At first it's all a big joke to William. Flashing the same wide grin that at other times is irresistibly charming, he gets Janine to chase him around one of the unwiped tables a few times. Not the least bit amused, she halts and says to him, "Listen, William, everybody has to help clean up here. So come on; it'll just take a few minutes if you quit messing around and get busy."

"No! I won't do it!"

When Janine closes in on William, he suddenly spits at her. "If you do that again, I'll have to sit on you," she warns.

William only laughs and then manages to get off one last goober before he finds out that Janine meant exactly as she said. Careful not to hurt him, Janine grabs William by both shoulders and lowers him to the floor. Then she glares down at him and says, "I'll let you up when you stop spitting at me and promise to do your job."

William keeps a smirking game face on for an impressively long time. Clearly, he's no stranger to passive resistance.

Solely in the interest of seeing the cleanup get done sooner rather than later—Janine is more than up to the challenge of dealing with William—I say to her, "Well, it looks like you may have to sit on him all afternoon, Janine. But don't worry, if you get hungry or thirsty, I'll bring you a little snack whenever you need one."

For dramatic effect, and with nods and winks between us

that William fails to notice, Janine and I discuss her favorite junk foods. This does the trick. William's stubborn posture quickly crumbles and he begins to thrash and yell with raging indignation. When the tantrum reaches its crescendo, William vomits, which immediately brings him back to himself. Like a kind big sister, Janine helps him clean himself up, and when she asks him again if he will do his job, he nods and heads straight for the bucket and sponge so that he can wipe off the table the rest of the crew has left for him.

Twenty minutes later I see William, for the first time, happily playing outside with a group of kids his own age.

Some may question my allowing—even encouraging—Janine to deal with William in such an abrupt, physical way. Wasn't being sat on by a much larger child unfair—perhaps even abusive? Absolutely not. Had I any sense that William was being harmed, either physically or psychologically, I would have intervened immediately. But it was evident to me that Janine was going only as far as she needed to limit effectively William's blatant disrespect for her. It was only after every attempt at reason had failed that she spoke to William in a language every six-year-old can understand, careful not to hurt him in the process. William, for his part, knew he was wrong and was relieved to be set straight so firmly and compassionately, as was evidenced by his genuinely happy demeanor immediately following the incident. I should note that William and Janine later became friends and he did his job more or less faithfully every week.

I should also note that children sitting on each other, which is a technique Free School founder Mary Leue came up with as a way for children to set limits with each other without anyone getting hurt, is not an everyday occurrence. It is a technique of last resort employed only with inordinately willful children who are in the habit of overstepping any and all reasonable bounds and is an effective alternative to the kinds of adult intervention to which such children quickly grow immune.

The significance of William and Janine's exchange is that William didn't butt heads with a rule or a policy, but rather with another person—whose response was not to punish or in some way label him. Instead, Janine insisted that he treat her with respect and then supported him in following through on his obligation. He came around so quickly, I suspect, because the person establishing the limit was another child, not an adult authority figure. This is why we have developed tools such as the council meeting system, which I will describe in detail shortly, to empower children to make their own rules and to discipline one another.

William's confrontation with Janine brings us to the critical issue of "structure." Sadly, the conventional classroom is now so crushingly saddled with standards and teacher-driven curricula that it has become a place of confinement where learning tasks are broken down into small, repetitive bits devoid of excitement or meaning, and where there is little room for individual differences. In such a setting, an energetic, highly intelligent, and capable child like William was bouncing off the walls from understimulation. To him the structure of his previous school was akin to a large cage where the teacher related to him as though he were some sort of wild animal whose impulses had to be constantly guarded against and controlled.

Meanwhile, a common misconception about our school—and about freedom-based schools in general—is that we are unstructured, or at least fail to provide enough of the structure that educators and psychologists proclaim so strenuously that all children need. What a great many uninformed observers don't realize is that the reason they can't perceive our structure is because they are looking in all the wrong places. When they don't see the desks, and textbooks, and all the other accouterments of structure to which our society is accustomed, they make the false, but easily understood, assumption that we have no structure.

Nothing could be farther from the truth. The Free School has a very definite structure; it's just that we try to keep it fluid and individualized so that we can attempt to meet the unique needs of every child. For instance, instead of a single standardized curriculum, we have fifty individual "curricula," each one based on the student's own interests and passions, as well as his or her own rhythm and pace. At the same time, we try to let individual situations and individual children dictate the necessary limits and boundaries, rather than relying on a set of predetermined rules and regulations.

Freedom, a cornerstone of our structure, means being able to chart your own course and negotiate your own terms. It does not mean getting to do whatever you want whenever you feel like it. That, as A. S. Neill—who founded a freedom-based residential school in England in the 1920s known as Summerhill —was careful to emphasize, is called license. Freedom always includes being held accountable for the effects of your actions on those around you.

The structure of the Free School, perhaps more than anything else, is a matrix of relationships—student with teacher, student with student, teacher with teacher. A great deal of the learning that takes place does so within those relationships. And many of the most important lessons end up occurring spontaneously, as in the case of young William above, and not according to a scripted lesson plan.

William, already a master of defiance, has suddenly found

himself thrown into dozens of new relationships with people of all ages. Each of these relationships will teach him something about himself and living in the world of others. And each will exert limits on his inappropriate behavior until he starts setting his own inner limits.

Ultimately, it is a school's structure that enables it to carry out its goals and purposes. Maintaining order, inculcating patriotism and obedience, cranking out an academic product as efficiently as possible, and competitively sorting and ranking children according to performance are the major aims supported by the structure of conventional schooling. At our school you will find almost the opposite to be true. Our first and foremost goal is to help children learn how to manage themselves and structure their own experience. Thus, we leave the school's time and space loosely structured in order to promote self-direction and personal responsibility, as well as to encourage cooperation and stimulate creativity and self-expression. Here we are far more concerned with fostering respect for self and the diverse world of others than we are with maintaining order.

The irony of the structure of the conventional classroom is that all too often it causes the very problem it was designed to prevent. When disorder is viewed as an enemy that must be fought off by structuring every moment of every day, it is virtually inevitable that spirited children such as William will fight back. Some do so overtly, as William did in kindergarten, by mouthing off and other forms of defiance. Others will engage in passive resistance by not paying attention, forgetting what they've been taught, and constantly losing their things.

In either case, the children who either can't or won't conform to classroom routine become the enemy, too, and the conventional classroom's response is increasingly resolute. If William were still in his old school, or in one similar, he would currently be on Ritalin and quite possibly other biopsychiatric drugs—whatever it would take to squelch pharmaceutically his boundless curiosity, his ardently self-centered point of view, and his creative ability to avoid anything he doesn't think he should have to do. The net effect of these so-called medications, an Orwellian term if ever there was one in this context, would be to internalize that school's structure. William would find himself in a chemical straitjacket, one from which even an artful dodger like him could not escape.

On the third day of William's trial visit I arrive at school without the dog. William detects the dog's absence immediately and calls out, "Hey, Chris, where's Lakota?"

"I couldn't bring her with me this morning because I had to go to a meeting before school," I reply. "Shall we go get her now?"

He smiles and nods all at once, and so off we go to fetch her from my backyard, which is only two hundred feet from the school. On our way back, we stop next door to visit the farm animals, which are housed in a small barn set back on two formerly vacant lots now belonging to the Free School community. We keep three goats, a rabbit, and a flock of laying hens for two primary reasons. One is so that our students, many of whom would otherwise never encounter any animals other than an occasional dog or cat, can learn basic animal husbandry. The other is that angry, flighty, antisocial kids are especially drawn to animals. The children feel safer with them and then are slowly able to transfer the affectionate connection they establish with the animals over to human beings.

After a few minutes in the barnyard, William, Lakota, and I head back over to school. This little interlude has given me the chance to ascertain whether or not William is harboring any ill feelings toward me for my support of Janine the previous day. We talk about how unpleasant it is to be sat on, but how it's not really the end of the world, either. It's clear to me that William has already put the entire incident behind him.

Back at school William resumes testing the limits of this exciting new learning environment that bears so little resemblance to his former school. Today he discovers the woodshop, where a couple of slightly older boys are already at work on a crude representation of a battleship that they are fashioning by themselves out of donated wood scraps from a local lumber yard. On the workbench rests a pictorial history of World War II, which has provided the inspiration for the project.

I explain the shop policy to William: Only kids who can be trusted are allowed to work in here without an adult. I conclude with the warning that the very first time he does anything unsafe in the shop he will lose his privileges for that day. He dives into the wood box as soon as I'm finished talking and pulls out the two biggest boards. Then, eyes ablaze with concentration, he begins trying to hammer them together with the largest nail he could find. On my way out, I close the door between the woodshop and my classroom in order to have enough quiet to continue reading my group the novel we started yesterday.

I keep one ear on the action in the shop because I'm less than optimistic about William's chances of handling the unsupervised freedom at this early stage of the game. But, I'm not overly concerned, either. There's been only one accident in thirty years, and that was when a young teacher cut his thumb while using one of the sharp handsaws, which we store elsewhere, along with other potentially dangerous tools, and which we let the kids use only when they're with an adult. Also, the two boys who are in there with William are both longtime Free Schoolers. I know they won't put up with any shenanigans.

After twenty minutes, my fears are confirmed. I hear one of the other boys in the woodshop shout, "William, put that hammer down! Didn't you hear what Chris told you?"

This is my cue to stick my head inside the woodshop door. "Hey, what's going on in here?"

"William started banging on our battleship with his hammer," responds Paul, whose voice was the one I had heard. "And then when we told him to stop, he waved his hammer around like he was going to hit us."

I give William a long, stern look and say to him, "Young man, hang up your tools on the pegboard and leave the shop right now! And remember you're not to come back in here for the rest of the day." He wisely puts up no protest.

Fifteen minutes later, however, I discover William back in the woodshop, hammer in hand once more. This time I make my message even plainer than before. "If I catch you in this shop again today, I will add another day onto your penalty and you won't be allowed to work in here tomorrow, either."

Again there's no argument, and this proves to be the last time William ventures into the shop that day.

Some may consider it foolhardy for a school to allow young children like William to work in a woodshop without adult supervision. It is, I admit, a policy we adopted only gradually as we discovered that kids can indeed be trusted to act responsibly on their own, or to police each other when one of them begins to get out of line.

There are several reasons why we do it this way. The first is purely logistical. We can't afford to hire a shop teacher, and if we required there to be an adult on hand at all times, then the students' use of the shop would be much more limited. Meanwhile, kids—particularly those prone to being labeled these days—need to be able to hammer and bang to their hearts' content. It is this kind of active, constructive release that keeps them from flying off the handle.

But even this isn't the most significant reason. In our guarded world of security police and surveillance cameras, it is more necessary than ever for children, even quite young ones, to have moments when they're *not* being watched, *not* being monitored. How else will they ever learn to act responsibly? It's the only hope for a child like William who is so heavily predisposed to getting negative attention from others. Until he begins to take ownership of his actions, and to weigh the causes and effects of the choices he makes against his own inner standards—so that his motivation to "be good" comes from within as well as from without—his connection with the world is not likely to be a terribly successful one. In any event, to try to restrain a willful boy like William with only external controls is a fool's errand. You would practically have to construct a special prison for children in order to succeed.

Besides, good teachers down through the ages have understood that the fastest way to turn around immature or irresponsible students is to give them an important task to accomplish independently and then trust them to do it right. My own third grade teacher, a thirty-year veteran by the time I reached her class, was a master of this little pedagogical secret. She knew just how to handle me, a child who probably would have been a candidate for Ritalin today. I used to finish my assignments light-years ahead of the others, and then my eight-year-old fanny would start to burn holes in my seat. During assemblies in the auditorium, I never seemed to be able to keep quiet or sit still. Finally, one day, when my best pal and I kept disrupting the film our teacher was showing, she suddenly pulled us from the room. Much to our surprise, we were placed in charge of the bookkeeping for the class savings bond program. That task, plus helping out in the textbook storeroom, became our job for the rest of the year. She had little trouble with either of us from then on.

It didn't escape me how William's eyes had lit up when I told him he could work in the woodshop whenever he wanted to, as long as he obeys the rules. There is little doubt in my mind that, probably with a few stumbles along the way, he will soon be able to muster sufficient resolve to behave in the shop. His desire to maintain his privileges will provide ample motivation. And should I prove to be right, it will mark the moment when William begins to invent a new self, one intent on seeking out experiences that nourish him instead of one determined to develop newer and better strategies for getting out of things or getting the better of others.

2

William manages to regain his woodshop privileges on day four of his trial visit and immediately begins working on a battleship of his own. Aside from hammering his thumb a few times, he completes the project without mishap. William is probably the only person on earth to whom his creation actually looks like a battleship, but then, that's not really the point. What is important here is that he made it without being monitored, and the end result was pleasing to him.

Meanwhile, however, there is other trouble brewing. William has started picking on a classmate who is only half his size. Thankfully, William seems to have a knack for choosing just the right target to best assist him with his education. Pierre, a diminutive French Canadian boy, refuses to play the victim even for a moment. With two older brothers, he learned long ago not to put up with any abuse from bigger boys.

Pierre does what kids usually do in our school when they find themselves being mistreated: He tells William in a loud, clear voice, "STOP IT!"

When William persists, Pierre takes the next appropriate step after someone violates the "stop rule." He calls a council meeting.

Council meetings are our all-purpose democratic decision-making plus conflict resolution mechanism rolled into one. And they are a great way to cure bullies. Pierre goes around the first floor crying out, "COUNCIL MEETING!" By prior agreement, we all stop what we are doing and form a large oval in what we call the "downstairs big room," a large rough-and-ready space that is also the home of the wrestling mat, punching bag, piano, and two large trunks filled with dress-up costumes. Three nominations are taken and a chairperson is elected. This time it is eight-year-old Abe, a compact, high-energy package who does such a capable job of running things that he is frequently chosen over much older candidates. Meetings operate according to *Robert's Rules of Order* and begin with the person who convened the meeting stating the problem or concern.

His small dark eyes shooting daggers at William, Pierre recounts three instances of William's bullying him.

William is given the chance to tell his side of the story but has nothing to say in his defense. He just sits and stares glumly into his lap. Immediately, young hands fly up around the room and William is hit with a barrage of indignant queries:

"William, why did you do that to Pierre?"

"I dunno."

"Do you realize how much bigger you are than him?"

"Yeah."

"Would you like it if I pushed you around or took your things?"

"Nope."

"Well then, why did you do it?"

"I dunno."

"Has anyone been treating you this way in school?"

"No."

"Does anybody pick on you at home?"

"My big brother does."

"Do your parents make him stop?"

"Sometimes."

Bullying is probably the worst "crime" anyone can commit in our school, and the kids have numerous ways to make it a regrettable act. Their peer-level justice can be stiff. This time, one of the older kids urges Pierre to make a motion that the next time William bullies any smaller student in the school, he will be sat on by that child, with the help of five or six other little kids. Such an idea must have been inspired by the Lilliputians' capture of Gulliver. It is a very effective deterrent.

Pierre decides to make the motion, which is seconded and discussed. The motion passes unanimously—William is too stunned by his sudden exposure to vote against it. For dramatic effect, Nancy suggests to Pierre that he choose his potential helpers right now, just in case William should forget and pick on him again. Hands shoot up once more. Pierre selects the rest of the kids in his and William's first grade class, along with one of the boys from my second grade class for backup. Someone asks Pierre if he feels that his problem is solved, and when he nods affirmatively, a motion is made to adjourn.

I am continually amazed by the orderliness of our council meetings. They stand in stark contrast to normal operating conditions in the school, which is like a highly charged molecule, its atoms dancing excitedly about an ever-shifting nucleus—or as Jerry Mintz, who started the Shaker Mountain School in Vermont, once said, "like Grand Central Station at rush hour." Mintz went on to point out that if viewed from the ceiling of that cavernous railway nexus, the apparent chaos actually contains a great deal of inherent order. Everyone more or less knows where he or she is going, and all eventually reach their destinations.

And if you were to spend sufficient time observing William or the other Ritalin kids in this book, you would see for yourselves, as educator/writer George Dennison wrote in *The Lives of Children,* that "the principle of true order lies within the persons themselves."[1] It generally isn't a neat and tidy kind of order. Oftentimes these children don't head in straight lines to their goals, but given the time, space, and trust to follow their own logic, get there they do.

It isn't long before William decides to test the will of the community again. In the van on the way back from apple picking—an annual rite of autumn at the Free School—he starts pestering Pierre, and when Pierre tells him to cut it out, William bops him painfully in the nose with a small bag of apples. So, immediately upon our arrival back at school, Pierre sets about carrying out the motion passed at the council meeting he called about William's bullying. He rounds up his already deputized supporters, and together they confront William, who has already begun playing in the downstairs big room. Taken a bit by surprise, William puts up only a mild struggle as they set him down on the rug as gently as possible. I stand nearby to make sure things don't get out of hand. When William finally wakes up to what is happening, he becomes furious and frightened all at once. He fights like mad to get free, but his six peers have little trouble keeping him safely planted on his back.

As soon as William runs out of steam and quits thrashing, Pierre, who is straddled across William's waist with a hand on each of his shoulders, looks intently down at him and says, "I just want you to stop bothering me, okay?"

No response.

"Are you going to stop?" Pierre tries again. "If you say yes, then we'll get off."

This time William's eyes well up with tears, and he says in a soft voice, "All right; I promise I won't do it again."

The kids immediately let William up and everyone goes about their business. It is important to add here that no one other than me was there to watch this process as it unfolded. Confrontations like these should never be allowed to become public spectacles.

The following day I happen to catch a snippet of an interaction between William and Pierre in their classroom. The two boys have the room to themselves and are working together on a puzzle. Apparently William has started to hassle Pierre, and from my classroom I can overhear Pierre saying to him, "Do you want me to sit on you again? If I have to I will!"

I lean out just in time to catch through the open doorway a look of recognition flash across William's face. It's a tough way to learn, but, as stubborn as William is, I think he's starting to get the message.

William has been with us on a trial basis a little more than a week now. Though he continues to do a lot of roaming, he gradually seems to be feeling more at home. This morning he told ten-year-old Carl he was going to call a council meeting if Carl didn't stop teasing him, a sure sign that William is catching on to how the system works. He busies himself in the woodshop for up to an hour at a time, and lately I've noticed him in there with Pierre building some sort of odd contraption. Perhaps there is a friendship brewing. Despite their physical and cultural differences, there is much they have in common. But I'm not sure William has ever had a real friend outside of his immediate family, meaning this is yet another crucial learning process that will take time.

This afternoon William agonizes over whether to go with me to pick more apples—this time at a commercial orchard that permits us to glean their unpicked apples for free—or go swimming with Nancy. He has even remembered to bring in his bathing suit and towel. William changes his mind at least five times while the two groups prepare to head off in their separate directions. His struggle with his dilemma is almost comical, but Nancy and I manage to contain our amusement and allow him the space to make up his own mind. At the last second, he chooses swimming, and he has a wonderful time at the pool. When I see William at the end of the day, he seems quite pleased with his decision.

Learning to make good choices is a fundamental prerequisite for leading a good life, and yet so many children, like William, have precious little opportunity to practice this all-important skill. The current hyperconcern with "standards" in American education is fast eliminating what scant room there used to be for choice in the conventional school day. And now the heat is on in the nation's day-care centers and nursery schools to push reading and writing on ever-younger kids. Homework, even at the pre-kindergarten level, is fast becoming the norm.

And the problem isn't only in school. In *Dumbing Us Down: The Hidden Curriculum of Compulsory Schooling,* John Gatto presents a time analysis of the typical American child's week.[2] He concludes that after you've added up the hours spent in school, as well as going to and from, plus homework, plus after-school activities such as music lessons or organized sports, plus meals and time spent watching television, playing video games, and on-line, a young person has only nine waking hours per week left to explore, imagine, and reflect. The equation varies somewhat according to social class, but the end result is about the same, says Gatto. That's all the time there is in which *they* get to choose what to think and do. It's simply not enough.

In addition, children's lives are becoming more programmed.

When I was a child the majority of our sports activities consisted of us kids organizing our own ad hoc games, whereas today there is an explosion of adult-organized leagues for every imaginable sport. There are programs for everything under the sun: before-school programs, after-school programs, special enrichment programs, summer programs, outdoor education programs, leadership initiative programs, and so on. Then, on the other extreme, there are growing numbers of semi-abandoned "latch key" kids who have far too little caring adult input in their lives, and, as a result, develop a deep disrespect for all forms of authority.

Kids also watched far less TV when I was a boy. Video games and personal computers didn't yet exist. The world was considered a much safer place for children, too, and I was pretty much allowed the run of the city of Washington, D.C., where I was born in 1954. Not so anymore. Safety is the name of the game wherever you go today, and kids' lives are becoming severely circumscribed as a result. Even ordinary play has been placed in tamper-proof packages, with the current proliferation of commercial play establishments. It's no wonder that more and more children have seemingly excessive amounts of energy, enough to earn them the label "hyperactive" and their parents a trip to the pharmacy for biopsychiatric drugs.

There's one more ingredient to add to this thickening pot of stew: The parenting style of my generation has turned out to be much more managerial than that of my parents' generation, and the trend seems to be ongoing, or even increasing, in the current generation of young mothers and fathers. So many parents I know are trying so hard to be good parents, to do the job correctly, better than their parents did. But there is a hidden cost in all of this parental conscientiousness. It is leaving kids with less and less opportunity to learn to work things out for themselves, to discover how to manage their own needs and rhythms. Wilhelm Reich called this crucial developmental task "self-regulation," a term he coined in the 1930s when he collaborated with A. S. Neill and others to formulate a model of healthy psychological development that would prevent the future need for the psychotherapy he practiced with neurotic adults.[3]

It all adds up to kids' making fewer and fewer choices all the time. And though I've never seen any scientific studies confirming my suspicions, I am convinced that there is a correlation between the rise of programmed childhood, with its lack of risk taking and choice making, and the exponential rise in the number of distressed children who have a hard time controlling themselves.

I get to meet William's dad at the parent conference following William's trial visit. Our policy is to meet with both parents if at all possible before children officially enroll in our school. There's no mystery where William gets his height. William Senior is at least six foot five and played college basketball in his home state of North Carolina. His hand engulfs mine when we greet each other.

Many fathers sit stiffly in their chairs and let their partners do the talking in these meetings. But this dad leans forward and fires off questions as easily as he used to shoot baseline jump shots. I can tell that he wants to believe in our unorthodox approach to education. The problem is he simply has no point of reference for the large degree of freedom we allow students, especially ones as young as his first grader. His initial questions echo his wife's earlier worries about whether or not William Junior will be able to master the basic skills when he has the choice to establish his own timetable for learning them.

It's so much easier when parents put their anxiety right out in the open. And it's a godsend when a boy's father elects to be this actively involved in the raising of his son. William Senior, however, was raised in the rural South, meaning that there is very little in common between his image of school and ours. I figure my best bet is to acknowledge this fact right off the bat and then to talk about the rising amount of fear our society arouses in parents as far as their children's cognitive development is concerned.

My one edge with this intelligent, concerned father is that he and his wife have tried the conventional school approach with both of their boys and it hasn't worked well for them. Nor, William Senior admits, did it work particularly well for him. "If it weren't for basketball," he says, "I probably wouldn't have made it to college."

Then Irene chimes in, "By the time I reached high school, I'd had it with being told what to do all the time. I went into a full-blown rebellion, one from which it took me years to recover."

Then both parents express almost in unison that they don't want their kids to have to go through the same painful transition into adulthood.

"If children are encouraged to think for themselves now," I add, "then the chances are good that they won't feel compelled to turn their adolescence into a combat zone."

I attempt to reassure William and Irene by recounting some of the high school success stories of recent Free School graduates. I emphasize that because our kids tend to develop such a strong sense of purpose and inner direction, they are better able to roll with the punches should they find themselves in a conventional high school situation. They have built-in "baloney detectors," a phrase I picked up from a younger friend. To them teachers are simply fellow humans, each with their own strengths, weaknesses, and idiosyncrasies. And for reasons unknown, many seem to have a real savvy for playing the grade game.

Here William Senior returns with an insight of his own: By placing so much emphasis on "building character," as he puts it, we not only prepare kids for future schooling but also help them get ready for life in the real world.

As in my earlier conversations with his wife, I can tell that I haven't entirely erased his doubts, but at least I have managed to spark in him the willingness to give the Free School a try.

The conversation meanders away from school issues and into matters of home and family. I get the sense that in their case Mom is the "nice guy" and Dad is the disciplinarian who issues the threats and does the spanking. Even though corporal punishment is part and parcel of the culture of the rural South, I express my disapproval of spanking as diplomatically as possible, arguing that the anger and resentment it engenders only tends to reinforce the behaviors the parent is trying to curb. I have already picked up that little William is a frightened child, and the image of him being reprimanded physically by his giant of a dad doesn't sit well with me. William Senior replies that he's trying to get away from spanking his kids and that they've begun to experiment with other disciplinary measures, such as sending the boys to their rooms or taking away their television privileges when they misbehave. Still, my impression is that punishment in one form or another is a major ingredient in their family life.

William Senior confides that he's usually exhausted when he returns home from his job delivering refrigerators and often doesn't have much energy left to give his sons. Irene mentions how she's always after her husband to spend more time with the boys so that she's not carrying the entire attention-giving load.

Pregnant with a third child, she has quit her job in order to take it easy and be more available to William and his older brother. Unfortunately, this means family finances will be especially tight for a while.

A few days after the conference with William's parents, my class and I decide on an apple butter project to raise money for a trip to an as-yet-to-be-determined location. Making apple butter will be a perfect autumn activity for the high-energy kids in my group because it involves lots of hands-on action. First the apples have to be quartered and simmered in a big kettle until they are soft enough to be mashed and run through a hand-powered food mill to remove the seeds and skins. Some of the apples will be rendered into cider, which will be used to sweeten and thicken the other apples as they cook.

We have borrowed an old hand-powered cider press for the cider making, which is a two-step process as well. Phase one consists of mashing up the apples with a hand-cranked grinder that is attached to the press, with the pulp automatically spilling down into a wooden barrel mounted underneath. Then a wooden block that fits snugly into the barrel is slowly driven downward by a large cast-iron screw. The kids love turning the big wooden handle and watching the juice flow magically out of the spigot.

William, who has been spending a lot of time with my group, has been a full participant in the process thus far. This morning he asks if he can accompany Lisa, one of my second graders, and me to the supermarket to buy canning jars for the apple butter. It's always a grand challenge to take an impulsive child like William shopping. Modern supermarkets contain so many inviting attractions, so many seductively displayed things.

Before entering the store, I put my arm gently around his shoulders and explain to him my rules: no running, no wandering off, no grabbing stuff off the shelves, and no begging me to buy him anything.

"I am willing to remind you once or twice if you forget," I add, "but after that we will leave the store without our supplies and go straight back to school."

Just to make sure he gets the idea, I help him to visualize the angry kids he will likely be facing if he is the reason we return empty-handed.

William quickly uses up his allotted reminders: "Chris, will you buy me some candy? Please!"

"William, what did I say to you about nagging me to buy you something?"

"Oh yeah."

When we pass by the aisle with the toys and games, William starts to dash down it. It's a case of the irresistible force and the immovable object. "Do you remember what I told you about staying with me in the store?" I call out.

I'm mildly surprised by his ability to break himself out of the toy trance and return to my side. We double-time it to the canning section, find what we're looking for, and zoom back to the check-out counter. I really want William to taste success the first time around.

On our way out I congratulate William for following my rules in the supermarket. But I push our luck too far when I decide to make a second stop at the lumberyard next door to pick up a repair part for one of the school's windows. I remind William about my store policy and in we go. Things probably would have proceeded smoothly if it weren't for the five-minute wait while the clerk tracks down the right hardware. The sight of all those power saws and drills is just too much for William.

Finally, when he just won't leave the merchandise alone, I have to resort to restraining him gently while the clerk and I talk over how to repair the window.

I should point out that I refrained from making an issue of William's behavior here for two reasons: First of all, he had no direct connection with the business I was conducting; and second, I was stretching him past his limits.

Nevertheless, my refusal to let William roam around and examine the tools and gadgets puts him into a sulk. After I pay for the window part, he refuses to accompany Lisa and me out to the car. My own daughters helped me years ago to discover the futility of getting drawn into power struggles with willful children in crowded stores.

"I'm going out to the car and driving back to school now," I say to William calmly. "Lunch will be ready, and I don't want to miss it."

With that I turn my back on William, who is still leaning against the counter with his arms wrapped tightly around his rib cage, and exit the store with Lisa. Fortunately, the car is parked right out front, so that William can see us open our doors and sit down. While I'm searching my pockets for the keys in slow motion, William suddenly appears by the passenger's side, where Lisa has already seat-belted herself in. Either hunger or the thought of being left behind has momentarily changed his tune.

But this blossoming minidrama isn't over yet. William's foot-dragging has enabled Lisa to beat him to the coveted front seat. He glowers at her and declares in a voice oozing with entitlement, "Hey, girl, that's my seat."

"No, it isn't," she replies with self-assurance. "You had the front seat on the way here, and now it's my turn on the way back."

Back go the arms across the chest. William is in no mood for fairness. He tells her no way is he going to get in the back seat. After a short pause, he starts to open Lisa's door with a look of determination that signals his intent to battle her for possession of the seat.

I generally don't like to intervene between kids in their territorial struggles over vehicular seating arrangements, but I for one am ravenous and have run out of patience with William's antics. Drastic measures are called for, so I shut and lock Lisa's door and say to William, "I'll give you thirty seconds to think it over, and then, if you don't get in the car, I'm going to leave without you."

William glowers at me as I begin my slow, ascending count. At twenty-five I turn the key in the ignition and rev the engine a couple of times for emphasis.

Then I announce: "Okay, William, time's up. Hope you find your way home all right."

Leaning stubbornly against the car parked next to mine, he still refuses to budge. It's a real standoff. But not for long—it's time to fight fire with fire. Sending him a determined look of my own, I shift the car into reverse and slowly ease out the clutch. That does it. As soon as William sees the car creeping back out of the parking space he cries out, "Wait for me!" I immediately stop and he opens the back door and climbs in.

Here, of course, I have broken the cardinal rule of effective limit setting, which is never to set consequences you're not fully prepared to carry out. I obviously wasn't going to drive off without William. But a six-year-old's fear of abandonment is almost always stronger than his will, and so I was fairly certain my bluff would have the desired effect. For those of you who might think it unfair to exploit a child's fear in this way, keep in mind that Ritalin kids rarely play by the rules either. They need adults around that are a step ahead of their game.

We go one more quick round over his seat belt and then

head back to school. Spying his still furrowed brow in the rearview mirror, I can tell his petulance isn't quite spent.

Sure enough, we haven't gone far before William begins to whine about not occupying the front seat. "It's not fair, Lisa; I had it first." To which he adds, "You're stupid."

Lisa wisely refuses to take the bait. After he repeats himself several more times, I can't help but ask, "Does your mother give in to you when you treat her this way, William?"

Smiling broadly, he answers, "Yup."

"Well, then," I return, "your mother is doing a foolish thing, because look at you now; you're six years old and behaving like a big baby just because you didn't get your way."

This launches him into a stirring defense of his mom: "She doesn't give in to me. I was just kidding." And then as an afterthought: "Don't call my mother foolish; she's smart."

"I know your mother's very smart, but she's making a big mistake when she gives into your whining and sulking. It's not good for you."

"I told you she doesn't!" he whines back.

I counter by turning to Lisa and asking her what she thinks.

Lisa, who along with her two older sisters was home-schooled until last spring, possesses wisdom beyond her years. She considers the question carefully and then answers, "I think his mother usually lets him win because otherwise he wouldn't be acting this way now."

Suddenly William changes the subject. "What are we having for lunch today?"

Kids as young as six, or sometimes even younger, are capable of an amazing degree of self-understanding. That's why I chose to engage William in the preceding conversation. I wasn't out to malign his mother but to get him to begin looking at the price he pays by trying to manipulate others with his sulking and pouting. William's essence is that of a proud warrior, not a whiner. It's not the way he wants to be in the world at all; it's just a typical child strategy that has paid off too often in the past. His mother, Irene, is, by nature, what we used to call "a soft touch." She doesn't want her boys to be angry with her, and so she probably has trouble holding her own in a busy supermarket.

While it never does much good to lecture young children, or to expect them to think and act like little adults, it is entirely appropriate to begin helping them understand the mechanics of their own behavior. They are generally more than willing to learn—provided the information comes from within the context of a caring, respectful relationship. Even though William tries my patience mightily, I genuinely like him. In no way was I trying to insult him by calling him a baby. Rather, I was holding up a mirror in which he could see himself in a new light, so that he might begin to exercise some choice instead of acting only out of impulse and habit. While I was being somewhat critical of his actions, at the same time I was communicating a respect for his ability to reconsider them and perhaps act differently in the future.

Herein lies the utter travesty, the flagrant inhumanity, of drugging children into behavioral submission. It is cowardly; it's a cop-out. It disregards their inborn desire to become whole persons. Given half a chance, the kinds of kids to whom medicalized labels are currently being applied in such wholesale fashion are more than willing and able to learn, grow, and change without someone altering their basic biochemistry.

To presume otherwise is to discount the human spirit.

3

Damian's mother telephones me in early November, not long after being told by the school psychologist in the public elementary school her son is attending to add another drug to the chemical cocktail she has reluctantly been giving him every morning before school. At this point he is up to thirty milligrams a day of Ritalin and yet, according to the school, it still isn't "working." The child's teacher continues to complain that ten-year-old Damian won't stay in his seat and that his mind frequently wanders from the assigned task.

This isn't the first time Paula has received "strong suggestions" from school officials about her son. When Damian entered kindergarten in a small-town public school, Paula was told almost immediately to put her son on Ritalin because, like William, he was exhibiting all of the usual "symptoms" of ADHD. Paula didn't at all like the idea of drugging her child, and said as much to the teacher and the principal.

The school's response: "Do it, or else we will file charges of child neglect with Child Protective."

Nothing strikes fear into the heart of a rural, working-class mother like the threat of having her child taken away by the local social welfare authorities, and so Paula gave in and began administering Ritalin. When she moved to the Albany area this past year, she hoped that the schools might be more progressive and permit Damian to come off of the drug.

Quite the contrary. Damian's new school was even more

intolerant of his restlessness, physical and mental, and proposed that Paula begin giving Damian the blood pressure medication Clonidine to augment the "effectiveness" of the Ritalin. Paula, worn down by the prior threats and the constant flow of negative reports about her son, gave in without a fight this time. Within days she received word from the teacher that, thanks to the new drug, Damian was a different child.

Here was the first good news this discouraged mother had heard from his schools in a long time. She eagerly looked forward to the upcoming Parents in School Day so that she could see the improvement for herself. When the much-awaited day arrived, Paula sat observing from the back of Damian's fifth grade classroom. She was nearly struck dumb with horror. The boy slumping heavily in her son's seat was not her son at all.

Paula decided then and there to find another option for Damian. She heard about us through the grapevine and was on the phone with me the next day.

"He was like a zombie, just completely zoned out," she reported, on the verge of tears.

"Damian will have to come off the drugs entirely before he can try out the Free School," I told Paula.

Our "No Medications" policy causes many parents to take pause. But not Paula.

"Do you really mean it?" she blurted out, incredulous. "You won't allow him to take the Ritalin and the Clonidine?"

"Absolutely not," I replied. "We find that kids simply don't need drugs here."

Paula arranged to bring her son in to begin his trial visit the following morning.

Damian's first day begins much like William's, except that Damian arrives with a ravenous appetite.

"I can't remember the last time I saw him eat like this," Paula remarks with obvious relief as we watch him wolf down a second bagel with cream cheese.

The next thing we know, Damian is bouncing on the minitramp next to the big mattresses, still chewing his last bite of breakfast.

Observing Damian, one is immediately drawn to his eyes. Their expression is intense, indicating perhaps an overload of energy. The dark circles underneath them suggest he hasn't been sleeping well. His complexion is soft and fair, a little paler than I would like to see this early in the winter season. When Damian takes off his pullover hat, the static electricity sends his medium-length brown hair every which way, giving him a comical look that doesn't seem to faze him in the least.

"Damian walks to a different drumbeat than the other kids," the principal of his previous school had apparently uttered to Paula in their parting conversation. "Perhaps he just doesn't belong here."

I, on the other hand, wouldn't call Damian's beat "different." It's just faster than most. He seems to do everything at a very high rate of speed. Today, for instance, he completes his first woodshop project in less than ten minutes. It's a tray for his mother, and the elaborate paint job he gives it takes no more than another seven minutes, including washing up the brushes. There is nothing sloppy about the finished product, either. Paula is delighted to receive it at three o'clock.

Damian is articulate and reads at well above grade level. A devotee of the children's interactive fantasy game Dungeons and Dragons—or "D and D" as he calls it, he regularly reads novels like *King Arthur and the Knights of the Round Table.*

Unlike William, who came in September, Damian has arrived well into the school year. It's always hard to be the only new kid, and so it's no surprise that he decides to spend a large portion of his first several days upstairs in the preschool with the little ones, where, understandably, he feels more secure. Damian alternates between amusing himself with our hybrid supply of toys and games and playing Pied Piper to the four- and five-year-olds. They are delighted whenever an older child shows an interest in them, and their instant glee is wonderfully confirming to him. The preschool teachers tell Damian they will allow him to hang out in their space as long as he isn't too rough or domineering.

After Damian has been with us for a few days, I find myself having an informal chat with him while he enjoys his usual postbreakfast romp on the upstairs jungle gym. He has reached the age when it isn't as easy for boys to connect with adults who are relative strangers, and thus far he has kept his distance from all of the teachers. We exchange general pleasantries and discuss his favorite movies and video games, but what I particularly want to know is if he's experiencing any ill effects from the sudden withdrawal of the drugs from his system.

"Are you feeling any different now that you're off the medications?" I ask him.

Damian ponders the question from his perch on the horizontal climbing ladder. Somewhat to my surprise he answers, "I think I feel a little calmer."

Though I don't want him to feel invaded, I can't help but press a little further. The Free School is anything but a calm environment. "Why do you think that is?"

After a thoughtful pause, he comes back with an equally unexpected response: "Because here I'm free."

Damian feels to me like a fundamentally frightened child. One can only wonder whether it is other people he is afraid of, or his own impulses—or perhaps some combination of the two. It strikes me that Damian's apparent inability to pay attention for very long, which was such an issue in his previous schools, is an expression of his being on the run from someone or something, and not a symptom of some organic disorder.

My intuition about Damian's fearfulness is confirmed when he accompanies a group on an expedition to a local goat dairy to breed one of our does. I had heard our doe Strawberry yelling plaintively out in the barnyard when I got up this morning, a sure sign that she is in heat.

With Strawberry on Lakota's leash, we all pile into the school van for the forty-minute drive into the country. I start the van and attempt to back out into the street, which is on a steep hillside sloping down toward the Hudson River. The van gets stuck. The rear tires spin hopelessly on a small patch of ice. Muttering a few expletives under my breath, I slouch down in the driver's seat and ponder my next move. Goats stay in heat for only twelve to eighteen hours, so it is imperative that we get Strawberry to her assignation with the buck as soon as possible. While I'm mulling over my options, Damian cuts through my private deliberations with a question of his own.

"Chris, can I go back to school now? I don't want to do this anymore." There is urgency in his voice and an anxious set to his brow.

Trying to reassure him, I respond in the calmest voice I can muster. "It's okay, Damian. It'll just take me a minute to get the van unstuck and then we'll be on our way."

I suddenly remember that I have a bucket of rock salt in my garage. A shovelful behind each rear wheel instantly sets us free, enabling me to keep my optimistic promise. But when I reach the city limits, I realize that in my haste I have forgotten the directions. It has been a year since my last trip to the goat dairy, and the finer details are a little hazy in my mind. I make the mistake of mentioning this out loud to Carl, who is sitting next to me in the "navigator's seat" and who accompanied me the last time we made this same trip. We agree that, together, we'll be able to recognize the way as we drive along.

But Damian has overheard our conversation. "Are we lost, Chris?" he calls forward from one of the middle seats. "I think I want to go back to school."

I tell him again that everything's fine, and we continue on into the late-autumn countryside. It occurs to me to distract Damian by suggesting to him that he watch for deer, which are often on the move this time of year. It's their breeding season, too. He doesn't see any, but the search keeps him occupied until I make my first wrong turn. Then the whole scene repeats itself.

"We're really lost, aren't we, Chris? Come on; I want to go back to school. Now!"

I decide to ignore his rising angst. At this point I figure my best bet is simply to get to the farm as fast as possible. I confer with Carl and we quickly locate the right road. We manage to arrive without further incident, and Damian's fears soon dissolve into the excitement of delivering Strawberry to her appointed rounds with breeding.

Monique, who has several grown children of her own and has been raising French Alpine goats for over thirty years, hears the van pull into the driveway and comes out of her house to greet us. After a round of introductions she leads us up the path and into the barn. On one end are three sturdily built stalls, each containing an adult male goat.

Monique tells us in a still-thick French accent that she is putting Strawberry in with the smallest of the three because of Strawberry's compact build. While the two aroused goats are becoming acquainted, Monique segues from an explanation of genetics into a delightful, age-appropriate sex education lesson.

There is plenty of giggling and face wrinkling for accompaniment, but Monique has no trouble holding the kids' attention as she explains the basic principles of procreation. Most of the group is so intent on her words that they miss out on seeing the goats' brief moment of consummation.

All of the kids, including Damian, are in high spirits on our return journey. However, the high level of insecurity our newest student is carrying within him has not escaped my notice. Here is a boy who has at some earlier point in his life been traumatized.

At the parent conference following Damian's trial visit, I learn one of the sources of Damian's deep-seated fear. When he was about a year old, his young mother and father separated permanently. Six months later, the dad found himself in a relationship with a woman who was a born-again Christian. This new partner, according to Paula, was extremely suspicious of Paula's pagan form of spirituality. She managed to convince Damian's dad that Paula was a Satan worshiper and that Damian was in great danger. So the dad kidnapped Damian one day and spirited him away to a neighboring state so that it would be more difficult for Paula to get him back again. After nearly a year of legal wrangling in the family courts of both states, Paula finally managed to regain custody of her son. But by then, she said, he was a different child. He was afraid to go places, or to be left alone.

"One way we can help Damian with his fear will be to expose him to it in small doses, like when I took him to the goat farm the other day," I tell Paula.

"Oh, I heard all about it from him when he got home," she

replies. "He must have talked about the trip for over an hour."

This is the standard approach to desensitizing children who suffer from allergies. It also lessens the grip of phobias.

I add, "Just being in an environment where there is no external pressure on Damian to succeed, or to socialize only with kids his own age, will slowly enable him to be more at ease, both with himself and with others."

The other important point I want to get across to Paula is that anger and rage very often accompany fear in the psyche. Although Damian has kept his angry feelings pretty much under wraps in school thus far, it is important for his mother to know that he is likely to begin coming out with them once he begins to feel at home here. Nothing has gone terribly wrong for him during his visit—no fights or major conflicts—and so this bridge has yet to be crossed. Paula needs to understand that the heart of the Free School's approach to fostering children's growth, especially kids like Damian who haven't had an easy time of it, is to help them learn to deal with their emotional selves.

"Given his history, I'll be amazed if Damian isn't sitting on a lot of unexpressed feelings," I continued, "so don't be surprised if one day he brings home a dramatic story of one kind or another."

We've learned over the years that it's always better to have this discussion with parents sooner rather than later, to avoid major upsets down the road.

"I know he's very angry and afraid on the inside, and after all I've been through with him, it'll take a lot to upset me," she assures me. "I can't tell you how relieved I am that he is in a place where people care more about emotional well-being than his sitting still and taking tests."

There is nothing naive about Paula, who is both thoughtful and forthright. It's much easier to address difficult issues with people like her who speak their mind freely. She shares that Damian is very stubborn and often gives her a hard time around issues such as bedtime and helping out around the house. She also shares that she has met a man in the area with whom she's now living, and that she is pregnant with her second child. She's very excited at the prospect of having a girl this time.

When I ask Paula for her assessment of Damian since he began coming to the Free School, her eyes well up with tears. "My God, you've given me back my son."

Child psychiatrist Robert Coles has spent the past four decades investigating how such factors as race, class, ethnicity, and family structure influence the emotional and cognitive growth of children. In the preface to the new edition of his book *The Mind's Fate: A Psychiatrist Looks at His Profession,* Coles laments contemporary psychiatry's steady drift toward substituting biological explanations for a subtler understanding of the internal mysteries of the human psyche. Emotional problems like those Damian is experiencing are increasingly seen as a disease of the body that can be "cured" with pills, just like a physical ailment.[1]

Thus, the field of psychiatry has begun to enter the brave new world of Aldous Huxley, where the only therapy is drug therapy. Huxley's soma now exists in myriad forms: one drug to remove depression, another to alleviate anxiety, and yet another to reduce excessive anger. While such a biopsychiatric approach was formerly limited to adult psychiatry, it is rapidly taking over the child branch of the field as well. Currently there are plans in the works to set up in-school mental health triage "clinics" in order to speed up the diagnosis of ADHD and others, as well as to prescribe the accompanying biopsychiatric drugs.

The bottom line is that fewer clinicians all the time are asking *why* a child like Damian might be chronically angry or anxious, have difficulty concentrating, or be impulsive or aggressive to the point of being unable to make friends or function in a cooperative setting.

Yet anyone who has spent time with children knows they are highly emotional beings, anything but predictable. When they are happy and in a state of relative emotional balance, they learn, interact socially, and accept appropriate authority with relative ease. When they are unhappy and out of balance, the opposite is true. To reduce a child's imbalance to a matter of faulty brain chemistry defies human reason. It's a shortcut to conformity. Though conveniently mechanical, it is unscientific, too.

Real science is beginning to validate the Free School's belief in the vital importance of attending closely to the emotional lives of children. The emerging field of neuroscience is confirming that emotions have a great deal of actual, and not just metaphorical, impact on human mental and physiological function.

For instance, Paul MacLean, a senior National Institute of Mental Health (NIMH) researcher in the Clinical Brain Disorders branch, has conceptualized a triune model of the brain that shows it to consist of three layers, one enfolded around another.[2] At the core is what he calls the reptilian brain, which promotes survival by providing information about the external world through the five senses. Surrounding the reptilian brain, the emotional brain monitors the interior environment, including the emotions and the immune system. The outermost brain layer is commonly known as the neocortex. It receives input from the other two brains and incorporates the data into overall growth and survival strategies.

Before MacLean's triune model, the neocortex, the center of cognition and memory, was the primary focus of attention. But it is now known that the emotional brain, which is appropriately sandwiched between the reptilian brain and the neocortex, maintains a constant neural relationship with the other brains and provides us with a sense of self, of reality, and of the continuity of ongoing experience. Quite likely, too, it is the home of our sense of right and wrong, and true and false.

More recently, researchers working in the new field of neurocardiology have discovered that the emotional brain also has a massive and direct neural connection to the heart, which, as it turns out, is far more than just an organ for pumping blood.[3] The heart comprises 60 to 65 percent neural cells, with a cellular structure similar in many ways to the brain. This means that the heart is not just metaphorically connected with the emotions, as was previously believed, but is an actual neural source of our emotional experience. It also means that, together, the heart and the emotional brain play a huge role in overall mental development.

One only has to get to know the stories of children such as Damian to begin to see the connection between their inner emotional states and their outward patterns of thought and behavior. Damian certainly isn't crazy, a fear he would later express in a self-portrait that is quite possibly a result of the damage done to his self-image by five years of labeling and drugging. He is a genuinely distressed child, however, and there are distinct, nonmedical, nonbiological reasons for that distress.

Damian's emotional makeup has an inner logic all its own. His family of origin underwent a violent disruption very early in his young life, and he remains separated from his father for all but a brief period each summer. Damian's dad continues to be a key figure in his life, and yet Damian's feelings toward him are tinged with ambivalence.

Ongoing power struggles have also been a regular feature of Damian's relationship with his mother, as is the case with many only-child/single-mother dyads. It is not uncommon for struggling single mothers to give in to the demands of frustrated and demanding male offspring. This dynamic contributes heavily to future patterns of impulsivity and resistant behavior.

In addition, having spent a majority of his childhood isolated with his mother, Damian is lacking in experience with either siblings or peers. When he is alone and left to his own devices, there is little about Damian that I would call a problem. It is living in the world of others where his troubles often begin.

Damian's first forays into the elementary section of our school aren't terribly rewarding, at least in social terms. On the surface he appears to have little sense of how to interact with other kids his age. He should, technically speaking, be in our teacher Dave's fourth, fifth, and sixth grade class—his date of birth places him right in the middle of that group—but thus far he is showing little interest in any of their classes, projects, or discussions. And his attempts at hanging out with these older kids seem always to leave him feeling like the odd boy out. Kids at this pre-adolescent stage have often already begun to adopt the tribal social customs of teenagehood, meaning that Damian certainly has a challenge in front of him if he wants to become a real part of Dave's group.

This afternoon, while the class is horsing around on the

wrestling mat in the downstairs big room, Damian has the first of what will prove to be his many run-ins with Carl. Carl is slightly older than Damian and has already been in the school for two years.

"Cut it out, Damian. You keep grabbing Larry around his neck, and I don't like it," Carl says crossly. Larry is smaller than Damian, and Carl is ostensibly concerned about his safety.

"I did not! I did not!" repeats Damian.

"Yes, you did," Carl returns, his volume rising. "I was looking right at you when you did it."

Round two is only a few minutes away. This time Damian has wrestled Vanessa to the mat.

"You better get off of her, Damian," warns Carl. "You've got no business picking on a girl like that. Do it again and I'm gonna kick your ass."

Damian's eyes momentarily flare with anger. It's no mystery what he's thinking. But, while Damian is larger physically, Carl has grown up in the inner city and has seen many a street battle. Damian wouldn't last thirty seconds in a fight with him. And Damian is nobody's fool.

To save face Damian says, "Why don't you mind your own business, Carl? I wasn't hurting her."

And so it goes for the remainder of the afternoon. Any signs of friendship between these two boys, who are so different and yet have so much in common, are presently beyond the horizon.

For the next several days Damian drifts through the school, more or less splitting his time between the upstairs and the downstairs. He lets on that he likes to draw, and so Dave makes crayons and a supply of large sheets of paper available to him. One morning he does several interesting drawings in rapid succession. The last in the series is a nearly life-size self-portrait. It has a cubist feel to it, with the figure split by a thick vertical line from head to toe. Each half is a different color. Scrawled across the top of the drawing are the words "I'm crazy."

Unfortunately, if Damian isn't engrossed in a creative pursuit, he gets himself in trouble. Nancy, Dave, and I begin receiving reports from the preschool teachers that Damian is being too overbearing with their little ones upstairs. At one point we hear that he put his hands around the neck of a five-year-old boy and shook him when he wouldn't go along with Damian's plan for a castle they were building together in the block corner. Apparently this wasn't the first time, so Dave takes Damian aside and explains to him gently, but firmly, that if it happens again he will lose the privilege of spending time in the preschool. Dave isn't encouraged when he gets back a blast of defensive argument and denial from his newest student.

It is Dave who witnesses Damian's next transgression. After lunch the following day, Damian is roughhousing on the mattress upstairs with a bunch of four- and five-year-olds. Dave has just finished eating at the teachers' table about ten feet away when he sees Damian grab another boy around the neck and begin to shake him vigorously.

"DAMIAN!" the ordinarily soft-spoken Dave barks. "I said you weren't to do that ever again. Now go down to our classroom and stay put until I get there."

There's no argument this time. Dave clears his place and heads downstairs to deal with Damian. Deciding it's time for some stronger medicine, he tells Damian that for the next three days he will be confined to their classroom, where all the kids are his age and size.

The following morning I can't help but laugh out loud when I walk into Dave's room to ask him about something. Dave and

Damian are alone, the teacher in an armchair with a look of bewilderment on his face and the student at the chalkboard busily coating his palms with different colors of chalk and filling the board with hand prints. The air is thick with the odor of chalk dust.

Still chuckling, I say to Dave, "Getting a little taste of public school teaching, eh? Imagine having to deal with this kind of captivity behavior every day."

"That's okay; I'd rather not," he says with a groan.

I direct my next question to Damian. "Brings back memories, doesn't it?"

"Yeah," he answers in a tone not unlike Dave's.

Feeling sympathetic about their sorry lot—the other kids have long since fled this dismal scene—I decide to sit down and stay awhile. I want to make sure Damian understands that the keys to his freedom are in his own hands.

"What do you think, Damian?" I ask. "Are you capable of controlling yourself around the little kids, or should the upstairs teachers just tell you to stay away?"

"I promise I won't hurt them anymore. Now can I get outta here?" he pleads.

"This isn't about promises," Dave interjects. "When the three days are up, the upstairs teachers and I will decide whether or not we want to trust you again. In the meantime you're gonna park yourself in here so that you understand the seriousness of what you've done."

Eventually Damian is able to drop some of his defensiveness. On the second day of his "sentence," he and Dave have a heart-to-heart talk about Damian's problem. Damian admits that he has trouble managing his temper sometimes, and that he forgets how much bigger he is than the preschoolers. He enters into an agreement with Dave that he will never again, under any circumstances, grab a smaller child the way he did. Sensing that Damian is genuinely ready to make a growth step in this area, Dave elects to give Damian a day off for good behavior. I don't know who is more relieved that the period of confinement is over.

In Damian's case, as with many Ritalin kids who aren't having trouble keeping pace academically, "undisciplined" behavior was the primary justification for labeling and drugging him in his previous schools. The question then becomes, What is the best way to respond to these willful kids who abhor control and resist it at every turn with such gusto and creativity, who have difficulty setting their own internal limits as well as accepting them from the outside?

One mistake many schools make is relying too heavily on standardized discipline. Preset rules and punishments, such as "time-out" chairs, and later, detention rooms, quickly lose their effectiveness. They seldom bring about any real change in a child's overall attitude or character. They reinforce anger, resistance, and resentment instead of fostering personal responsibility. While they may reduce certain out-of-bounds behavior in the short run, over time they create students who feel they have no share or ownership in the school or the educational process. It turns what could be an important source of teaching and learning into a control issue, and in the end it creates alienated students who simply don't care anymore.

All of this is not to say that what we generically call "discipline" is not an important issue, both in school and at home. It is critical for teachers and parents alike to establish a baseline of respect for necessary limits, and to be able to stop kids effectively and nonabusively when they cross that line. Abuse is so often an act of desperation when nothing else is working to limit an out-of-control child.

Good teaching in school—which invariably involves a measure of parenting—and good parenting at home are delicate dances that involve creativity and improvisation. However, in school the issue of discipline is endlessly complicated by the large amount of coercion attached to the learning process. Teachers are thrust into a vicious cycle of dealing with the reactions of certain students—the highly energetic boys, and sometimes girls—against being forced into a daily regimen that runs counter to their basic natures. Then the teachers react to the kids' reactions, and a vicious cycle ensues. The same negative pattern repeats itself when parents attempt to enforce the school's academic requirements at home.

At the Free School we automatically eliminate half of the problem by removing compulsion from the learning process altogether. Next, we try to stay out of the business of behavioral management, allowing kids to learn from their own mistakes when at all possible, because mistakes contain within them important opportunities for self-discovery. We prefer natural consequences over fixed, predetermined ones. For example, kids who forget to bring their wet bathing suits home after their weekly trip to the public pool are greeted the next time with that same moldy, damp rag wrapped in plastic. If they want to swim badly enough, then that's what they will have to wear. It's an error seldom repeated. Or, as in a case such as Damian's that clearly calls for adult intervention, we establish consequences that follow logically from the out-of-bounds behavior. Because Damian has been mistreating smaller children, Dave told him he couldn't be around them, and that he would have to make a commitment to changing his ways before he could enjoy the liberty of playing with the preschoolers again.

We presented Damian with the chance to take a look inside himself and reflect on his actions. Middle childhood is certainly not too soon for a boy to begin engaging in self-examination. He got to see for himself how angry he is, and was confronted and then given the opportunity to choose whether or not he wanted to try to handle his anger differently in the future.

Even though Damian's misdeed was a very serious one, Dave's response was not to punish him in some formulaic way. Rather, it was to confront Damian with the full heat of his disapproval without shaming him or demanding blind obedience, which would only have driven Damian's hostility further underground. Then Dave made sure to follow up with a caring presence in order to give Damian a chance to reestablish the trust on which the freedom in our school is based. Confining Damian to his classroom for two days was not the Free School's standard penalty for bullying. Dave didn't get the idea out of a handbook on discipline. Instead he followed his instincts as to how best to deal with an individual boy in a particular situation.

In the end, Dave's decision to release Damian from the confines of the classroom was based entirely on Damian's response to the question "Can we trust you to act appropriately around the little kids, to remember how much bigger you are than them, and to control your temper?" When Damian answered "Yes," Dave had to rely on his intuition again to determine whether Damian really meant it. The idea behind letting Damian off a day early was to end the affair on a positive note and give Damian a boost in the right direction.

Damian, a little gun-shy after his confinement with Dave, chooses to remain downstairs on the first morning after his release. He flits in and out of my open-to-all-ages math class like a hummingbird. On his first flight in he requests an arithmetic workbook (from a programmed, self-teaching series that I'm fond of and the kids seem to like). He proceeds to do a few pages in rapid succession; then he's off again just as suddenly as he arrived. When I call after him to put his book away, he yells over his shoulder, "Don't worry, I'm coming back to do some more." True to his word, Damian returns several times, and by the end of the session he has probably accomplished as much as most of the others. Because the students are all proceeding independently at their own pace, his transient learning style poses no problem as long as it doesn't disturb the rest of the group, which it didn't seem to today. When I check his hastily completed work at the end of class, I find no mistakes.

The following morning Damian brings in his Dungeons and Dragons materials: an elaborate game board that he has constructed, reference books, and a slew of plastic swords, shields, and body armor. Before long, my entire group of second and third graders is crowded around him, asking if they can play. Lex, who is the seventh and eighth grade teacher and was once a D&D devotee himself, helps them get organized. Swords and shields are distributed, roles are assigned, and then Lex quietly disappears as soon as things are more or less established. The game proceeds with amazing order, and the kids are reluctant to stop when lunch is served.

The action resumes immediately following the noon meal. To my total surprise, Carl is now one of the players, too. A stranger to the game, he willingly accepts Damian's knowledgeable direction and quickly gets the hang of it. This marks a significant turning point in their relationship.

D&D remains the rage at school for a week or more, with Damian as maestro throughout. One morning he comes into my algebra class and asks to borrow all of the chairs we aren't using. When I inquire what for, he answers that he's holding a class on D&D in the big room. Twenty minutes later, I slip out of my class and into his, only to find him seated in front of a group of six students lecturing on the various medieval creatures and entities around which the game revolves. He has their rapt attention. The class doesn't break up for at least another twenty minutes.

When Damian finally reemerges in the preschool, he appears to have a new role in mind, that of entertainer. He asks Missy, one of our preschool teachers, if he can break out the large supply of puppets she keeps on hand. Fresh from his teaching success downstairs, he has decided he wants to put on puppet shows for the little kids. Missy is only too happy to oblige, and before anyone quite realizes what's happening, Damian has converted her kindergarten worktable into a makeshift puppet theater. He ad-libs his way through a zany rendition of slapstick comedy that he improvises on the spot. The kindergarten fills with raucous laughter, and word of the performance quickly spreads throughout the upstairs. Act II plays to a standing-room-only crowd. Before long, audience members become actors and Damian seems perfectly pleased with the circus he has set in motion. He welcomes all comers, and there is very little squabbling over who gets which puppet.

Suddenly Missy can be heard saying about this youngster who had been such a problem only a week before, "What a gift he is!"

Damian's interest in puppetry leads to the kindling of a friendship between him and Andrew, our newest intern, who works weekends as a professional clown. The son of Eastern European dissidents, Andrew, like Damian, definitely marches to his own drumbeat. The two hit it off squarely, spending hours together over the next several days, writing out elaborate scripts for future puppet productions. Andrew is only nineteen and has been with us just two weeks, so I think he is relieved to have already established a close rapport with one of the students. This means that Damian is making yet another valuable connection to his newfound community.

Here is the very same boy who less than a month before had been found by his horrified mother slumped at his school desk, driven into a drug-induced stupor by a system that had no appreciation for his gift of imagination, no tolerance for his frenetic, idiosyncratic personality, and no compassion for his rancorous vulnerability and damaged sense of self.

Which is not to say that we have "saved" Damian by any means. He still has a long, bumpy road ahead of him, a lot of wrong turns yet to make. His vehicle is already dented and scratched, a hubcap missing, the shock absorbers worn from potholes previously encountered. His engine idle is still set a little bit too fast, and his trunk is loaded down with baggage. But his sense of direction seems true enough, and there is sufficient reason to believe he has within him all that he will need to complete a successful passage through this life, though no one, including Damian, knows exactly where he's headed.

4

Carl, like William, had a narrow escape from being labeled and drugged. But Carl managed to find the Free School entirely on his own last year. He was exploring the neighborhood on his bicycle late one summer afternoon, having just moved here from across town, where he had been attending a large, predominantly African-American elementary school. The move was fortuitous because Carl had been having serious problems in school, both behavioral and academic. Had the teaching staff there not been so overwhelmed by the number of students and the severity of their needs, he likely would have been labeled and drugged by the time he showed up at our doors.

When Carl dropped in that day—the doors were open because the teachers were inside getting ready for the upcoming school year—he was, as most neighborhood kids are, a bit dubious about the sign out front with the word "school" on it. He asked if he could look around, and his doubts were confirmed by the absence of many of the traditional trappings—rooms lined with desks, long hallways, and heaps of textbooks. It wasn't long before he asked, as they always do, "Is this a real school?"

Then after an affirmative answer, he asked, "Can I go here?"

To which we replied, as we always do, "Go home and talk to your mother. If it's all right with her, then it's okay with us."

Nine times out of ten the kids don't return. But in Carl's case he was back within the hour to tell us his mother said he could come. We informed him that school would start the following

Monday at 8:15 and to please bring his mother with him so that we could meet her and she could fill out the necessary papers to launch his trial visit.

Show up he did, with his mom, Odaisha—and his five-year-old sister, Lamika. Unbeknownst to us, this was going to be a two-for-one deal. Odaisha had few questions about the school's philosophy and seemed unconcerned by its unconventional, somewhat funky appearance. She was simply glad to have found an alternative to the public schools, where neither Carl nor his much older sister, Pearl, had ever experienced much success, as well as a school to which both of her younger kids could walk safely.

When Carl arrived at our school for fourth grade, he exhibited numerous signs of the mental and emotional trauma he had experienced in his previous school. Whenever he got too close to anything that smacked of traditional schoolwork, he reacted as though he were allergic. On certain rare occasions I could entice him to participate in low-pressure math games that I sometimes play with the kids, especially the ones who don't respond well to conventional teaching methods. But as soon as he didn't immediately know the right answer, his typically brash expression would disappear and his eyes would dart around as though they were scanning the room for the nearest exit.

Carl's father left the household soon after Lamika was born, and Odaisha was frequently out of work. The older sister, Pearl, had dropped out of high school, joined a local street gang, and become the source of frequent crises at home. The responsibility for taking care of Lamika, then, fell largely on Carl, cutting sharply into his freedom to roam and play after school—a source of resentment for him.

Like William and Damian, Carl is highly active and energetic. He is deeply frightened, too, his fear rooted in the violence, betrayals, and unpredictability of ghetto life. He has seen too much already. And like all distressed children, he acts out his disturbed emotions in a variety of ways.

This was especially true in his first year with us, when the primary vents for his emotions were fighting and stealing. He had an explosive temper, and even though he was small, he didn't hesitate to escalate an argument into a physical altercation. If someone called a council meeting because of his behavior, the whole experience represented to him a diminishment of his masculinity.

So how did we deal with Carl's anger and violence? The key word is *gently*. Whenever we saw Carl getting ready to blow up, someone—preferably one of the men—would sidle up next to him, gently put an arm around his shoulders, and soothingly say something to him like, "Carl, I know you feel like beating Jimmy up right now. It's okay to *feel* like doing it. We all get really mad sometimes. But it's not okay to actually do it. That will hurt Jimmy, and it will also hurt you because you'll feel bad about yourself afterward."

For some months, Carl's response usually went something like, "I don't care. I just want to mess him up."

The good news was that Carl was open to being soothed when he was upset, so that if one of us sat and talked with him long enough, he would usually calm down and forego his aggressive impulses.

Meanwhile, even though Carl refused to call his own council meetings at first, the rest of the kids didn't hesitate to do so when Carl threatened them. This meant that others didn't have to suffer from Carl's wrath unless they too were spoiling for a fight.

It was our volunteer teacher Jeff who was able to reach Carl best. Jeff, who later joined our paid staff, would take him for long rides in his red Pontiac sports coupe, a last vestige of his career as a highly paid restaurant chef. Carl loved to go fast and delighted in this one-on-one time in the car with Jeff. A mentor relationship quickly developed, providing Carl with a supportive context in which he could reveal his feelings of vulnerability and begin learning how to hash out his problems verbally.

By the middle of his first year at the Free School, Carl's temper had begun to subside. However, as so often happens, as soon as you close one vent another one opens. In place of fighting, Carl started stealing. What a prodigious thief he was. And a damned clever one, too. Suddenly the other kids' money and toys were disappearing on a daily basis, or so it seemed. The victims called council meetings to address the problem, but no one ever admitted to the thefts, even though confessions are cheered and the thief is not punished. There were few clues pointing to the guilty party. The other teachers and I suspected Carl from the outset, but we never caught him red-handed and his alibis stood up to scrutiny. Moreover, he always had a plausible back-up explanation in his hip pocket should anyone manage to shoot a hole in his first story. I'm thankful few children can lie as coolly and convincingly as Carl.

Finally one morning Carl slipped. All the elementary-age kids had brought in three dollars to go to a play at a local children's theater. About a half-hour before it was time to leave, seven-year-old John discovered his money was missing from his cubby. He promptly called a council meeting, at which I, suspecting Carl once again, immediately made a motion that we cancel the field trip unless the money was recovered. My motion carried, and then someone else moved that we postpone the meeting in order to conduct a thorough search of the building.

Lo and behold, it was none other than Carl who found the missing cash. The meeting reconvened and Carl announced that he discovered the money behind the toilet in the upstairs bathroom. Then John raised his hand and said, "But I didn't go to the bathroom upstairs. I put my money in my cubby as soon as I got to school."

The suspicions that had been growing around Carl came pouring out. "How come you thought to look in the preschool bathroom?" someone asked.

"I don't know. I just did."

Then several kids reported seeing Carl downstairs for the entire duration of the all too brief search. A poll of the assembled group yielded no one who had seen him go upstairs to check the bathroom. Next one of the boys asked for permission to check with the preschool teachers to see if any of them had seen Carl come upstairs.

When he returned and reported that none of the preschool teachers had seen Carl, I decided it was time to pop the big question. "Carl, did you take John's money? You know that if you admit you did it nothing bad will happen to you. John already has his three dollars back and we will still have time to make it to the play."

"I told you I found the money in the bathroom behind the toilet."

"But there's no explanation for how it got there."

"Somebody probably stole it out of John's cubby and hid it there."

"And no one saw you go upstairs to find it."

"I hate you people. No one ever believes me."

Carl was starting to unravel, but the clock was ticking and there was no confession in sight. Not wanting the kids to miss the play, Nancy made a motion that a court be convened to decide Carl's innocence or guilt, complete with judge, prosecutor, defense attorney, and jury. There was no precedent for such a proceeding; however, council meetings are vested with the authority to create new policies. After a brief and excited discussion—during which time Carl's face grew steadily darker—the motion passed unanimously. A trial date was set for two days hence to allow time for the attorneys to prepare their cases. The council meeting was adjourned just in time for the kids to make it to the theater.

Fortuitously, the seventh and eighth graders had been away on an overnight trip on the day of the theft. When they returned the next day, the judge, a sixth grader, appointed them jurors—a perfect choice because they knew nothing about the case. Meanwhile, the prosecutor gathered evidence and Carl's lawyer met with him to help construct a plausible defense.

The trial was an epic event. Carl entered a not guilty plea, and his attorney did an excellent job of pointing out that all of the evidence against her client was circumstantial. The prosecutor came up with little to add to the damning facts that had emerged during the council meeting, but the jury, after deliberating for nearly an hour, found Carl guilty as charged.

Interestingly, there was no protest from the defendant.

The judge then asked for a recess so that he could come up with an appropriate sentence. When he returned he ordered Carl to spend one week doing community service in the school kitchen helping the cook prepare lunch. Again there was no protest, and Carl went on to serve his sentence cheerfully. When the week was up, the cook made a point of telling Carl that she would miss him.

Several months later, in another council meeting over a stolen item, Carl—fortunately not the culprit this time—finally admitted to the earlier theft of John's money. He then proceeded to help the current perpetrator take responsibility for his actions and lead the meeting to a happy conclusion.

Children have an internal guidance system. In Carl's case, somewhere in his eight-year-old mind he knew that the school where he had attended the first three grades was not the right place for him and that it was time for a change. In fact he confided to me after he had been with us for a few months that he had been able to feel his third grade teacher's unspoken racial prejudice toward him. And so, magically, mysteriously, he was "guided" to a new school, one where he would have the opportunity to work out the kinks in his character and discover the side of himself that can allow him to set a positive example and be a leader among his peers.

While modern Western culture tends to balk at the notion of inner guidance, other cultures past and present believe in such things. For instance, the ancient Greeks called it the *daimon*, which they imagined as a kind of combination inner mentor and directional compass that urges a person to fulfill his life's purpose. Socrates reported that his *daimon* actually spoke aloud to him when he was faced with difficult choices. The Romans picked up on the same idea and called it the genius. Christianity has kept it alive to the present day, albeit in a much reduced fashion, in the form of the guardian angel.

In his book *The Soul's Code*, psychologist James Hillman, a student of Carl Jung—who also believed in the *daimon*—takes the idea of the *daimon* and weaves it into something he calls the "acorn theory."[1] This theory, as the name implies, is that, just as an acorn contains within it a fully developed oak tree, so every infant enters the world with a fully developed internal image of his or her destiny, as well as with an already delineated life purpose. It's very much the opposite of Locke's belief that every newborn is a *tabula rasa,* a blank slate that the child's environment then molds and shapes into its own image.

Child development is not a process of programming children as though they were new computers just off the assembly line, Hillman says. Rather, each child comes into the world already equipped with his or her own unique program, and development then becomes a matter of the child's discovering and unlocking the program, with some sort of *daimon*-like inner principle providing impetus and guidance.

Hillman is also saying that there is a fine line between his acorn theory and the ideas of fate and predestiny. Nothing about a child's development is predictable or predetermined. Sometimes the environment will support the realization of one's reason for being; sometimes it will hinder it. Many parents and teachers today, notes Hillman, make the mistake of confusing themselves with the child's *daimon.* They presume it to be their job to direct their children toward their children's goals and dreams, not realizing that such adult interference, however well meaning, can make it a Herculean task for the *daimon* to fulfill its mission.

The idea that children are born equipped to guide themselves through life has yet to be verified scientifically—it remains confined to the realm of metaphysics—but I have seen enough demonstrations of this phenomenon in action over the years to know it to exist.

Which isn't to say that children don't need external guidance from time to time, because of course they do. But at the Free School we try not to confuse guidance with the management, control, surveillance, and indoctrination that underlies the conventional educational model. Carl, as you will discover, will continue to receive mentoring from Jeff, who is helping Carl to learn that there are options open to him other than acting out his anger through fighting and stealing. And the council meeting system will always be there to guide Carl back into the fold when he has wandered.

We will respect Carl's preference for going it on his own, knowing that his mistakes will be some of his best teachers. We will allow him the space to encounter learning on his own terms. And above all, we will honor him for who he is at his deepest core rather than coax him toward our image of who we think he ought to be.

This year, Carl continues to show few signs of engaging in anything resembling legitimate schoolwork. His mother, though, seems to be satisfied, because both of her kids can't wait to get to school in the morning and she no longer receives troubling reports from her son's teachers.

Carl remains quite small for his age. Although his mood still swings between a steely seriousness and carefree abandon, he is steadily gaining control over his angry impulses. When he is amused, his laugh sounds like a cross between a witch's cackle and the staccato drumming of a woodpecker. He shows all his teeth when he smiles.

What Carl lacks in size, he makes up in guile and tenacity. This year he is the alpha male of Dave's fourth, fifth, and sixth grade class. It is a large group, eleven kids in all, with a few more boys than girls. And neither Carl nor Damian spends much time interacting with it. Very much a lone wolf, Carl has staked out the downstairs big room as his turf. He tends to spend a good deal of his time there, engaging in a wide variety of physical pursuits.

Carl and another student, Vanessa, also ten, have been steadily developing an intense love/hate relationship. Both have a penchant for showing their obvious affection for each other with various forms of verbal and physical aggression. The interaction always tends to follow the same course. It begins with the kind of teasing, laughing, and name-calling that has become a cultural staple among inner-city preadolescent boys and girls. This mode of relating in and of itself would be no big deal. Both parties join in freely and eagerly, and both seem equally adept at one-upping the other. The problem is that the verbal sparring invariably escalates into a physical altercation, with each party, if he or she gets mad enough, capable of doing real harm to the other. Thankfully, either or both are usually willing to call a council meeting before the confrontation reaches an advanced stage. Thankfully, too, Vanessa is an eager student and spends a sizable portion of her day engaged in academic pursuits, meaning that she and Carl aren't together all that much.

One afternoon, Vanessa calls a council meeting after Carl pushes her against the blackboard in the downstairs big room. Vanessa's back apparently struck the metal ledge that holds the chalk and eraser, causing a minor yet nonetheless painful bruise. Vanessa begins with a lengthy, blow-by-blow description of the confrontation. The chairperson has to call Carl to order several times when he loses his composure and blurts out, "That's a lie," or "I *never* said that!"

When Vanessa is finished, someone asks Carl for his side of the story. Not surprisingly, Carl's abbreviated version differs from Vanessa's on several key points. Before he can complete his last sentence, Vanessa, her head shaking audibly from side to side, thrusts up her hand so that she can continue the argument.

The chairperson, an eighth grader this time, is all too familiar with the pattern. She refuses to call on Vanessa and instead asks if there were others in the room and, if so, could they please tell everyone what they saw and heard. Two witnesses share eye-witness reports, both of which point to Vanessa as the instigator of this round. She had come into the room and immediately begun teasing Carl about his unruly hair, which has grown quite long of late and which he had unbraided the night before. Her calling him "Nappy head" led to his calling her "Fatty," which led to both of them making disparaging remarks about each other's mothers, which guaranteed that pushing and shoving would soon follow.

"I know you didn't like it when Carl hurt your back, Vanessa, but you started the fight. So what do you want to get out of this council meeting?" another eighth grader asks astutely.

"He always be pushing me. I just want him to stop."

"But you made fun of his hair, and then you cracked on his mother."

"I was just playin' with that boy."

"Isn't that always how trouble begins between you two?" interjects Dave. "You start out 'playin',' and the next thing you know you are both really mad and ready to fight."

Neither Carl nor Vanessa looks at Dave; nor will they look at each other. It's an all too familiar impasse.

I try to think of something to say that will lighten up the situation. "You know, when I was ten and I was attracted to a girl, the only way I could think to let her know was to tease her."

Several of the kids who have been in the school for a long time roll their eyes as if to say, "Here he goes again with another one of his stories." Others giggle and start to squirm in their places.

"And then I would keep teasing her until she decided she didn't like me anymore," I continue, deciding to keep this one short and sweet. "I wonder why I did that?"

No one elects to take up my question, least of all Vanessa or Carl, whom I can just barely hear muttering under his breath, "I *don't* like Vanessa." Across the circle I notice that the corners of Vanessa's mouth have turned slightly upward, hinting at a smile.

A couple of students and teachers attempt to get Carl and Vanessa to engage in some form of conflict resolution, but it quickly becomes clear that neither is ready to give up the game. Finally in frustration—there have already been numerous council meetings over this issue—someone makes a motion that Carl and Vanessa have to stay away from each other for a week. The motion won't solve anything between them, but at least it will send them the message that the community is losing patience with their unwillingness to change the way they treat each other.

Meanwhile, William and Damian are busy doing their share to keep the school hopping. Today Missy comes downstairs to call a council meeting because William has pushed down one of her three-year-olds while he was playing up in the preschool. William ran away when Missy attempted to talk with him about the problem, and Missy wisely elected not to chase after him.

Once again William has little to say for himself. He sits staring straight ahead, his face exuding an angry guilt. From the reports of others who saw what happened, it appears that William had a quick-tempered reaction to something that the little boy said to him.

The other kids are just as hard on William as they were on Damian earlier. Someone makes a motion that William be banned from the upstairs for two weeks. During discussion of the motion, Damian, sensing an opportunity to be on the right side of the law for a change, is the one who is able to penetrate William's stony defenses.

"Listen, William, I know I've been a real jerk with the little kids," he says earnestly, "but I don't think I'd ever hurt a three-year-old."

To which he adds, "You need to find some other way to get mad."

Damian's first stab at peer counseling seems to be having an effect, as William turns his head toward him with a look of recognition. William slowly raises his hand, and after he is recognized by the chairperson he replies, "I know I shouldn't a did it."

"Why did you do it?" asks William's classmate Pierre.

"Because he called me 'stupid' when I wouldn't give him the red truck."

Again, Pierre: "Why didn't you tell him to stop?"

"I was too mad."

"I know how much you love to come upstairs and play with the little kids, William," Missy says, "and we like having you. But you have to start telling them when you're angry. You're too big to be pushing them and hitting them. Do you understand?"

William nods remorsefully in Missy's direction.

"Do you think you can remember the next time to use your voice instead of your muscles?"

William nods again.

"That's good. Because if you forget and get too rough with anyone upstairs again, I think we will have to tell you that you have to stay away for a while."

The group, satisfied that William means what he says, votes out the motion to ban him from the upstairs by a substantial margin.

Damian, meanwhile, has gotten another flurry of D&D activity going with the boys in my group, who are now all carrying loose-leaf binders filled with pencil and marker sketches of the characters each has invented for the next game. Today they spend the entire morning together drawing, comparing notes, and designing a new game board. Damian makes occasional suggestions and comments regarding the latest creations of the others, while at the same time he continues to add to his own voluminous collection. Damian had better watch out that he doesn't become too overbearing, because this group is a collection of leaders, not followers. Even though Damian is at least two years older, they're going to give him only so much leeway.

I'm impressed by the boys' level of concentration, as well as by the quality of their drawings, which, even though they are producing them in large quantities, have a high degree of detail. I'm grateful to Damian for introducing this new activity, because several of the boys in my class are highly energetic and might well have been labeled, too, had they wound up in a conventional school setting. Art is an excellent way to entrain restless minds and foster the capacity to maintain focus, a requirement for reading. And I'm especially delighted that the figures the boys are drawing have absolutely no connection to the television action heroes that otherwise tend to dominate their fantasy lives.

I locate a book of Arthurian legends in the school library and decide to spend the next several mornings reading out loud to the boys while they draw. The mood is perfect for them to lock in on these tales of enchantment and heroic exploits. Damian, already well read in this area, flits in and out of the story sessions much like he did during the earlier math lesson.

On Friday, Damian announces it's time for the D&D game for which they've been preparing all week. The boys ask if they can take over our classroom, and I head off to teach algebra to some of the kids in Lex's class.

I return after an hour to find the classroom empty and the

D&D group scattered throughout the school. When I come across one of them and ask how the game went, he answers morosely, "Damian was being too bossy and so everybody quit."

A few days later Damian infuriates Carl by using his remote control car without his permission. It's not the first time Damian has played with the car when Carl wasn't around. Today he has managed to crash it into a table leg, causing slight damage to the body. When Carl threatened to do much worse to Damian, Damian wisely called a council meeting to save himself from bodily harm.

In the meeting Carl's classmates succeed in calming Carl down enough to get him to speak to Damian.

"How many times have I told you not to touch my car unless I say it's okay?" Carl shouts, nearly in tears. "You're always messing with people's stuff."

"Carl said he was gonna kill me," Damian responds with tears of his own. Followed by, "I hate you, Carl."

One of the older kids intervenes. "When are you going to get the message that Carl doesn't want you to touch his car without asking him first?"

Without raising his hand Carl interrupts: "My father gave me that car, and I'll be in trouble big time if he finds out anything happened to it."

As to the question of why he keeps playing with Carl's car without asking, Damian answers, "Because every time I do ask, he always says no."

This time Carl waits to be recognized by the chair. "That's because I'm always catching you messing with it. I'm sick of you, Damian."

Dave decides to wade into the middle of this infinite regress. He steers the discussion in the direction of what Damian can do to make amends for the damage to Carl's car. Ultimately,

Damian offers to try to repair it, and Carl is satisfied, at least provisionally, with this as a solution to his problem. Fortunately, it turns out the only trouble with the car is that a fender has been jarred loose. Damian is able to snap it properly back into place with little difficulty. Unfortunately, the incident has done little to bring the two antagonists closer together.

A key component of Damian's education this year is interpersonal relationships. There is nothing wrong with his mind or his basic academic skills, but he simply has no clue how to make friends. Instead of ADD, perhaps Damian and Carl have FDD—friendship deficit disorder.

If only biochemists could concoct a drug to cure people's inability to enter into genuine intimacy with one another. But there is no such remedy in sight; nor can such a thing be taught. No, it can be learned only through the trials and tribulations of daily interaction. What Damian and Carl are suffering from is a deficit of experience with peers, not some supposed genetic incapacity for getting along with others. Due to troubled childhoods and several unhappy, unsuccessful years in public school, both boys have already developed a series of coping mechanisms that inhibit intimacy. What they need now, more than anything else, is the time and the safe setting to practice the art of human relating. Because the Free School is a community as much as it is a school, the experience they need will be available in abundance.

Carl and Damian are far from alone in their predicament. It is through prolonged contact—and inevitable conflict—that kids learn friendship from each other. But because modern-day schools keep kids so busy and under constant surveillance, because so many contemporary families live in isolation from one another, and because the activities that do bring kids together, such as sports and recreation, are so heavily orchestrated, a great many children are deprived of the opportunity to connect with one another in the informal ways that enable them to form real bonds.

Damian and Carl are caught in a vicious cycle. Their abrasive ways of reaching out repel other children, and the ensuing negative feedback leaves them unhappier than before. Their increased frustration then leads to even more intolerable behavior, and around the circle they go. If there were a pill that could pull them out of this downward spiral, I would be hard pressed to oppose such a shortcut.

At the Free School we have yet to find any such instant answer to the social difficulties of distressed kids. All we can do is make social development an integral part of school life. The reason we place so much emphasis on it is that children who are secure in their relations with one another are happier and more confident. And happy, confident children progress more quickly toward their true purpose and their full potential. The formula is that simple.

Achieving this goal, on the other hand, is not so easy. All the school can do is to facilitate the process by creating a safe, caring environment in which the learning can occur. The first step is perhaps the most crucial. Teachers remove themselves from the center of the action and resist the ever-present temptation to mediate children's experience, especially when there is conflict. Instead of adult-centered control, we have the council meeting system, whereby kids can work out their differences by communicating honestly with one another and inventing their own solutions. Teachers are present as coparticipants, not as managers. Certainly we are there to guide and to advise—the children respect the natural wisdom and authority that stems from our greater experience—but only when necessary. The lessons that kids learn on their own or from one another are often the lifelong ones.

The process takes time, however. It is often ambiguous, full of steps forward and steps back. At this point Carl and Damian are in an intermediate stage where they are openly expressing their dislike for each other. The rest of us need to be patient and wait for future opportunities to help them discover how much they actually have in common. Though they live in vastly different worlds, they share the same vulnerability. Both have difficulty entering into genuine friendships with their peers, and both favor situations and relationships where they can be in control. Clearly these two wounded boys have much to teach each other, but only if they are allowed to do it in their own way and in their own time.

5

Thus far you've met William, Damian, and Carl. Now let me introduce you to three other boys who have taught me so much about how to help distressed children thrive and flourish without resorting to stigmatizing labels and mind- and mood-altering drugs.

Brian entered our seventh grade in the middle of the school year after having been diagnosed with ADHD at the late age of eleven and taking Ritalin for more than a year. His previous school, located in an affluent suburban school district, had been pressuring Brian's mother, April, to have him "tested" since he was in the third grade. The school suddenly became insistent after his sixth grade teacher complained repeatedly that Brian spent too much time clowning around and was unable to keep up with the rest of the class. April still didn't like the idea of putting her son on a biopsychiatric drug, one that he might never get off, but the school's dire forecasts about Brian's future frightened her so much that she finally agreed to have him evaluated. Then, after he was labeled ADHD, she reluctantly began administering Ritalin to him every morning before school.

When Brian arrived at the Free School, he was quite articulate about the effects of Ritalin on him. He hated the experience from the start. Ritalin made him jittery, irritable, sometimes ready to explode with anger. His outward freneticness had simply been shifted inward. The drug, Brian told me, catapulted him from a resistance to concentrating in class to an almost obsessive attitude toward his schoolwork. Once a master procrastinator and the class clown, he now vehemently shooed away his friends until he was finished with the assigned task. But he derived no satisfaction from his newfound "ability." Rather, he felt chained to his desk and did the work only because he had no other choice.

The worst part, Brian said, was when the drug began to wear off. As soon as he returned home from school, the volcano that simmered just beneath his skin would erupt all over again. He bounced around the house, or in good weather the neighborhood, until suppertime, when he would pick fitfully through the evening meal. He seldom ate much anymore, because Ritalin left him on the verge of nausea most of the time. Food had lost most of its appeal.

The drug's most profound effects on Brian, however, weren't the physical ones. Taking Ritalin, he believed, marked him as different—at a sensitive point in his development when no child wants to stand out. It meant that there was something wrong with him, or in his vernacular, that he was "dumb." Before long he discovered that he didn't really like himself.

Brian eventually began feeling so oppressed by the drug that he frequently hid the pill under his tongue and spit it back out when no one was looking. It was the strength of such protests that led his mother to look for alternatives, and that ultimately brought him to the Free School.

Just like that of Damian's mother, Paula, April's relief was instantaneous. Dosing her son every day with a powerful psychostimulant had aroused a great deal of maternal guilt. Deep inside she knew that Brian wasn't defective, that he was simply more energetic and restless than most, enamored with being the center of attention. She could see that Brian was highly intelligent but that he just wasn't expressing his intelligence in typical left-brained ways.

Brian is a brash, likable boy with a trace of freckles and a ready smile. He loves to tease and joke, and his quick, playful energy has made him a favorite of the preschool kids. It is nearly impossible for him to walk through the upstairs without at least several of them shouting out, "BRIAN!" while latching on to one or another of his lanky appendages. When he isn't rushing off to do something, he will stop and play patiently with them for half an hour or more.

Brian has boundless physical energy. He's very athletic and is a star player in a suburban youth basketball league. In the time that he has been with us he has relaxed somewhat, but he still has little patience for the slow pace of academic work. He reads sufficiently well—a mark of his perfectly adequate intelligence—but we seldom, if ever, see him sitting down with a book. His greatest passion appears to be people. Neither gender nor age seems to be a critical factor, though he tends to spend the majority of his time hanging out with his early-teen classmates.

This year Brian has formed a particularly close friendship with Tyrone, who has just come to the school from the slums of New York City. Tyrone is also an excellent basketball player, and the two boys can often be found honing their skills on the court up the street from the school. The relationship extends outside of school as well. They trade overnights at each other's homes and frequently get together on weekends. It's a beautiful cultural exchange. Brian is busily introducing Tyrone to suburban middle-class culture, something that was a galaxy away before he moved to Albany, and in return Tyrone is teaching Brian the latest in ghetto slang, music, and dance. Both mothers are very fond of their "second sons."

It is not an exclusive relationship, however. At one time or another Brian can be found fooling around with just about everyone in the school. Very recently he and Michael, a sixth grader born in Jamaica, worked out a zany duet in which Michael carefully captures a large, fat bumblebee with his bare hands and gently holds it still while Brian slips a loop of sewing thread around its belly. Then the boys take turns "walking" the bee around the school on its leash. Before the bee becomes too exhausted, they take their not entirely willing pet back outside and set it free again, unharmed.

The trick sends people reeling with laughter and is one of those things you have to see to believe. I suggested to the boys that they write a letter to *Late Night* host David Letterman and offer to perform it on his television show. It's just the kind of weird stunt the offbeat talk show host might go for. A born show-off, Brian jumped at the opportunity, and for the past two days he and Michael have been sitting shoulder to shoulder at one of the computers, trying to figure out how to pitch their idea to Letterman and doing an Internet search to find out where to mail the letter. Knowing Brian, I won't be surprised if the show calls him.

Brian was neither imagining nor exaggerating the way Ritalin made him feel while he was taking it. Nor was he alone in his experience. In *Talking Back to Ritalin,* psychiatrist Peter Breggin cites numerous scientific studies conducted over the past decade that point to the widespread physiological and psychological side effects of Ritalin and the other psychostimulants.[1] One of Ritalin's most common side effects is the suppression of growth due to the disruption of growth hormone cycles. Ritalin interrupts pituitary function and growth hormone production. Not unlike appetite suppression—which the drug also causes—growth hormone disruption impairs the growth of all the organs of the body, including the brain. This is because Ritalin hampers the body's ability to metabolize glucose—the brain's only food—and decreases overall blood flow to the brain by as much as 30 percent. In one 1986 study, an Ohio State University researcher found shrinkage of the brain in 50 percent of the young adults who had been taking stimulants since childhood.[2]

Ritalin is known to alter brain biochemistry in other significant ways as well. It increases dopamine, serotonin, and norepinephrine levels and causes the loss of receptors for certain neurotransmitters. It also disrupts the reticular activating system in the brain, a key player in an array of neurological processes that govern our ability to take in new information and then contextualize it into learning and awareness.

And these are only the physiological changes wrought by the continued use of Ritalin and other stimulant medications, the implications of which are only beginning to be understood. There is a long list of psychological side effects as well. Psychostimulants, writes Breggin, commonly cause a wide variety of psychiatric symptoms, including apathy and depression, obsessive/compulsive disorder, insomnia, agitation, and in extreme cases, mania. Moreover, as the drug wears off between doses, behavior commonly rebounds to a more extreme level of hyperactivity than before the drug was taken.

Perhaps most significant, psychostimulants suppress a whole range of spontaneous, self-generated, exploratory, playful, and social behaviors. They produce docility, passivity, social isolation, and sometimes a robotic or zombie-like conformity. Even psychologist Russell Barkley, a longtime Ritalin proponent, noted in a study of twenty "hyperactive" boys that stimulant drugs "reduce a child's interest in social interactions."[3]

A recent NIMH study reported that two of the more chemically potent stimulants, amphetamine and methamphetamine, can cause permanent, irreversible damage to the brain in the form of actual brain cell death.[4] The study went on to reveal that serious adverse drug reactions occurred in at least 8 percent of the study subjects, and when looking only at the incidence of drug-induced obsessive-compulsive reactions—such as nervous tics and preservative behaviors—researchers found a rate of 51 percent.

And then there is the more amorphous but no less significant issue of stigmatization. Peter Jensen, chief of the NIMH research branch for children and adolescents—which ardently defends labeling and drugging nonconforming kids—conducted a highly instructive study while he was an army base psychiatrist in a special ADHD clinic at Fort Gordon in Georgia. Because the test subjects were all offspring of army personnel, their medical records were unusually extensive and complete.

In this study, Jensen asked twenty children and their parents a series of in-depth questions about the ADHD treatment process. He also had the kids draw a set of pictures, one of the pill they took, one of themselves taking the pill, and one of their families.

According to a brief summary of the study in *Science News,* Jensen concluded that children on Ritalin often perceive themselves as "bad."[5] As a result, they suffer a loss of self-esteem that in some cases is considerable. Jensen also found that the children studied often disavowed responsibility for their behavior and claimed they need a "good pill" in order to control themselves. Moreover, the parents of the medicated children tended to avoid dealing with family conflict and to ignore the emotions underlying their child's behavior. They expected the drugs to resolve their child's behavioral difficulties.

"Indeed," concluded Jensen in another report, "the presumptive diagnosis of Attention Deficit Disorder seemed to prevent further careful attention to other factors that either contributed to or exacerbated the child's dysfunction and current difficulties."[6]

Even though Breggin and Jensen are currently foes in the pitched battle raging over the use of biopsychiatric drugs with children, here Jensen has Breggin's full agreement. One of the most insidious side effects of the drugs, Breggin believes, is that they allow adults to control children without attending to their genuine basic need for play, exercise, rational discipline, unconditional love, and engaging, individualized, and developmentally appropriate education. I couldn't agree more.

Meanwhile, count Brian among the lucky ones. He was blessed with the fighting spirit to resist being labeled and drugged, and with a mother who believed in him enough to listen when he said enough was enough. Now he can look forward to a drug-free adolescence and the chance to be just like his peers. All he needed was a school that honors his natural gifts and allows him to structure his learning around them.

Walter is another fortunate boy whose mother's instincts prevented him from being labeled and drugged. He came to the Free School five years ago from the publicly funded magnet school on the uptown edge of this neighborhood, when his second grade teacher insisted that he be tested for ADHD. Walter was apparently spending so much time daydreaming in class that he wasn't keeping up with the rest of the kids. There were no problems with Walter's behavior, the teacher had said; he just seemed to be a little "slow."

Walter's mother, Carol, was still upset when she called me.

"There's nothing wrong with my son," she yelled into the phone before apologizing. "He reads above grade level and is glued to his computer at home, always trying to find out about all kinds of stuff. I know I'm his mother, but really he's very smart. I just think he's so bored in school that he's lost interest."

Walter's first few weeks with us confirmed his mother's assessment. What we saw was a precocious, curious youngster who already read fluently and whose brain was bursting with information on just about every subject you could imagine. There was a certain know-it-all-ness that wasn't likely to endear him to his peers, and a certain oddness, too, from his eclectic interests, his somewhat rumpled appearance, his wacky sense of humor. Nowhere, however, did we see any signs of a genetically based chemical imbalance in his brain.

What Walter's former teacher perceived as slowness had, I think, been correctly diagnosed by Carol as boredom. Walter wasn't slow, at least not mentally, or even dreamy. He was what I would call a bit aloof at times. An only child when we met him, he often preferred his own company in school and had no trouble blocking out the buzz all around him so that he could engage in various solitary pursuits, his favorite of which was, indeed, surfing the Internet. He liked to sit for long periods and read books, especially scary novels, making him a teacher's dream in my opinion, considering his age and gender. Had I the opportunity, I would order ten more boys just like him.

At first we were concerned that Walter might have social difficulties here. But we quickly realized that when he wanted to connect with others, he would. He was quite friendly, actually; it was simply that his penchant for sedentary activities set him apart somewhat in the high-energy atmosphere of the Free School. It didn't take long for him to become an accepted member of his peer group, even though he was way ahead of many of the others intellectually, and literally way behind all of them physically. Whenever we would go out on walks, it was Walter who would pull up the rear, and he always finished last in games that involved any running. It wasn't that he didn't try. He was just too heavy. Here lay our only concern about Walter—he was overweight to the point at which it might adversely affect his health as he got older.

Now Walter is eleven. He has sprouted up, and, while still high, his weight is at least better distributed. And he still has the same engaging smile, all dimples, when he is particularly pleased with one of his own oddball jokes.

Walter also continues to be a thoughtful, perceptive child who, in addition to having a head full of facts, now has opinions about a great many things. He doesn't hesitate to share them, either, and his outspokenness is making him a real student leader. What one particularly notices about Walter is his highly developed sense of justice. In council meetings he frequently makes attempts to help resolve disputes, and he carefully weighs each proposed solution to make sure it is fair to all concerned.

Walter has seemed a little low lately, more serious than usual. And upstairs in the preschool his little brother, Rudy, who began coming this year, has been very temperamental. Last week he gave one of his playmates quite a bite on the arm. Missy called Carol and learned that both Carol and her husband have been struggling with health issues. As a result, the household has been under a lot of stress. Information like this is always helpful, because now we can make sure to cuddle Rudy and sit with him in our laps more, and look for opportunities to encourage Walter to talk about how he's feeling.

Walter is a perfect example of a child whose alleged "problem" was entirely a by-product of the failure of the school environment to meet his individual needs. Walter wasn't the problem, in other words: his classroom was. The harried teacher, mandated to keep all of her charges on the same page at the same time, couldn't allow Walter to follow his own idiosyncratic learning path even if she had wanted to. She couldn't permit him to spend two uninterrupted hours reading a good book from cover to cover, or to postpone memorizing his addition and subtraction facts until he was in the right mood for that kind of repetitive, left-brain exercise. "Time on Task" has become the mantra of every school district across the nation.

The interesting thing to note is that I have rarely noticed Walter daydreaming since he has been in our school. Not that there is anything wrong with daydreaming, mind you; it's a perfectly natural and acceptable activity. I have no doubt that geniuses like Albert Einstein and Thomas Edison did quite a bit of it in their youth, because daydreaming can be a profound source of inspiration. In Walter's case, however, I think his daydreaming in his former second grade classroom was a form of passive resistance to the mental oppression he was experiencing. It was his only available escape.

Walter feels little need to daydream now because we make every effort to live up to what A. S. Neill, founder of the Summerhill School, said: "The school should fit the child and not the other way around."[7] I think Neill would be pleased at the way Walter's self-designed curriculum fits him to a T.

On that note, I should add that these days a great many homeschooling parents with children who were previously labeled ADHD in conventional school settings are discovering that the "symptoms" magically disappear after they remove their kids from school and allow the learning process to unfold in a more organic and individualized way at home.

So, no, Walter is not a problem here. Quite the contrary. I never see him at a loss for something purposeful and interesting to do. I never see him misusing the freedom and trust we extend to him. I never see him trampling on the rights and sensibilities of others. Again, I'd welcome ten more just like him!

Which brings me finally to Mark, who, like Carl, managed to avoid being labeled ADHD by exiting stage left before the system could get a fix on him. His mother and father brought Mark to us in the middle of his first grade year in his neighborhood public school because he was showing little evidence that he was learning anything and was beginning to lose interest in going to school at all. The parents, an African-American couple in their late forties who both work full-time, brought him to us because they hoped Mark would benefit from the generous individual attention that our students receive. Reasoning that their older, already grown children had all had unsatisfactory experiences in public school, they decided to try a different approach with their youngest—already struggling academically just as his siblings had.

We always hope that by removing coercion and boredom from education we will cause students to fall in love with learning. It very often happens this way, but it was hardly the case with Mark, at least not in the beginning. Like William, he initially decided to take full advantage of the freedom of choice offered to him and to spend the majority of his time playing. On occasion Nancy was able to coax him into some brief reading lessons, but each time his progress was minimal. Mark was exhibiting all the signs of what used to be referred to simply as dyslexia. There was the classic reversal of *b*s and *d*s and difficulty tracking the letters from left to right. To make matters worse, Mark would forget the sounds he worked so hard to commit to memory the previous day. He failed to build on what he was learning in his one-on-one sessions, so that for him reading was like Sisyphus's pushing the stone up the hill.

It wasn't that Mark didn't try. At least part of his brain was attempting to focus in on the rows of confusing symbols. But after fifteen or twenty minutes of diligent work, he would lose heart because, even with Nancy's patient, expert teaching, he wasn't able to break the code. Understanding his predicament, she didn't prolong the agony but instead would praise him for his efforts and send him on his way. After a while, he stopped wanting to try altogether, and Nancy knew not to push him because that would only generate resistance and add to the size of the task.

Every once in a while Mark would express interest in doing a little math, and so I worked one on one with him like Nancy had. He seemed to grasp the concept of numbers well enough, and how to add and subtract them, but just as with the reading, his inability to remember facts and patterns from one day to the next made his progress painstakingly slow. I've seen this same phenomenon in other boys Mark's age. It's as if the left side of their brain, which handles memory and sequential thinking, is in a dense fog. The answers are out there lost in the mist.

In my experience the fog will usually lift on its own, although it depends on the cause or causes. If the cause is emotional distress, then it is first necessary to take steps to alleviate it. Mark didn't exhibit any signs of serious distress in his first months at the school, and so the reasons for his disconnected memory and fuzzy problem-solving ability remained a mystery.

In any event, Mark was a clear example of a child who was simply not ready to engage in the cognitive steps that reading and math require. And while this was a matter of some concern, we at the Free School have found it far more advantageous to relax and wait for better mental weather than to push children prematurely and risk turning learning into an onerous chore—damaging their self-esteem in the process.

What Mark did fall in love with almost immediately was another boy in his class. Bert had entered the school a couple of weeks before Mark, and the two hit it off right away. Before long they were practically inseparable, during and after school. Because Bert was an only child, his mom, Laura, was delighted that her son suddenly had a bosom buddy. She told Mark and his parents that Mark was welcome at her house anytime. Mark's parents, having already been raising children for more than twenty years, were more than happy to oblige.

Mark's transition into the Free School proceeded relatively smoothly, until he showed up at school one morning flashing a twenty-dollar bill. Having a naturally suspicious mind that dates back to my own larcenous youth, I asked Mark where he got the money. His response that he had found it on the front steps of the school didn't ring true. He had a kind of vacant expression on his face that left me wondering.

So I mentioned the incident to Nancy, Jeff, and Dave and suggested that we all check around to see if anyone was missing twenty bucks. When no one came forward, I decided to go back to Mark. "Are you sure you found that money on the steps? I have asked everyone in the school if they lost twenty dollars and they all say, 'No.'"

"Well, actually, I spent the night last night at Bert's house, and Laura gave it to me," he answered with the same vacant look.

"Wow, that's a lot of money," I returned. "Why'd she give it to you?"

"I don't know. She didn't really say why."

I decided I'd better act fast before the cash disappeared and Mark had a problem he couldn't easily repair. Fortunately I was able to reach Laura by phone and tell her Mark's story. "I've been looking for that money all morning," she said, her voice rising. And then, "You know, this is the second time he's stolen money from us."

"Well, I'm glad we caught on to him so quickly," I responded. "I will speak to him here and then hold the money until three o'clock, at which point I'll return it to him so that he can return it to you and apologize when you come in to pick up Bert."

Laura's English accent suddenly got stronger. "What shall I say to the little bugger?"

"Certainly tell him how you feel about what he's done. And then if I were you, I would tell him in no uncertain terms that he won't be welcome in your home if he does it again."

Her next question: "Why do you think he did it?"

"It's a red flag. Kids who steal are usually upset about something that's not right in their lives," I answered. "How has it been going when he's with you?"

"Everything's been fine as far as I can tell. Mark is very polite and cooperative, and he and Bert have been getting on famously."

"Well, maybe something's up at home. I'll go find him and talk with him now."

I located Mark, and we found an empty room where we could talk in private. "Listen, Mark, I spoke with Laura. I know that she didn't give you that twenty-dollar bill, and that you took it off her kitchen table," I began.

It's always best, when you are reasonably sure that children have done something wrong, not to try to pry a confession out of them. It only puts them in the position of telling further lies and makes it even harder for them to take responsibility for their actions.

"Now, I want you to know that Laura likes you very much

and she's glad that you are Bert's friend. So what I want you to do is let me hold the money for you until school is over so that nothing happens to it. Then I will give it to you so that you can give it back to Laura when she comes to pick up Bert."

I saw no trace of that vacant look. "What are you going to say to her?" I asked.

"I'm gonna say I'm sorry."

"Good. Are you going to steal from her again?"

"Un-uh."

"Make sure to tell her that, okay?"

"Okay."

I had one more question for Mark. "How is everything at home?"

"Fine."

I wasn't expecting a substantial answer. As is often the case with young children, the important information isn't contained in the words; it is in their expression. Mark's vacant look had cast a shadow across his face again.

The restitution went as planned, and to the best of anyone's knowledge Mark never stole anything else from Bert's house.

But it was only a matter of days before Mark came in one morning waving around another large bill—a fifty this time. One of Mark's classmates ran to find Nancy and alert her. "Nancy! Mark has FIFTY dollars!"

Nancy and I had a quick back and forth and agreed, even before we knew all the facts, that it was time to call in Mark's parents for a conference. I volunteered to probe Mark about his latest acquisition.

"Wow, Mark, where'd you get all that money?"

"From my dad."

"Does he know you brought it to school?"

"Yeah."

"I really don't want anything bad to happen to it while you're in school. Why don't you let me hold on to it until it's time to go home."

"Okay."

This time Nancy took on the parent phone call. She reached Mark's mother, Sheila, at work, and Sheila confirmed the obvious: Her husband did not give fifty bucks to their son. She confided that she had been wondering lately whether Mark was stealing small amounts of change at home, and she agreed with Nancy about the need for a conference posthaste.

Nancy and I met with Mark's parents early the next evening after Mark's father finished his job as a warehouse manager. Bill's eyes were tired and impassive, and he sat well back in his chair throughout the meeting. Sheila did most of the talking.

Nancy's and my goal here was twofold: to help these two appropriately concerned parents understand that when children this age steal, it's usually a cry for help of some kind, and then to try to figure out what that cry might be about, together. When Nancy asked Sheila and Bill if there had been any significant changes at home recently, both initially shook their heads from side to side, but then Sheila offered that she and her husband had both been working a lot of overtime lately so that they could catch up on their bills. This left Mark home alone a lot—when he wasn't visiting Bert, which was more and more becoming the norm.

In front of her husband, Sheila told us that she was always urging Bill to spend less time in front of the television and more time with their son, but that her nagging did no good. Bill, now on the defensive, sat forward and said that he was exhausted when he got home from work and that television was his way of winding down. He also claimed that when he asked Mark if he wanted to do something fun on the weekends, Mark often told him that he had already made plans with his friends. To this Sheila commented, somewhat bitterly, that it was a sign Mark had given up on his dad.

And so went that revealing, and disturbing, conference. It was the first of several over the course of the next two years as we tried to address Mark's unmet emotional needs. Thankfully, his string of outrageous thefts ended as suddenly as it began, but other warning signals popped up in its place. Various people began reporting seeing Mark roaming the streets far from his home at all hours, sometimes alone, sometimes with a group of urchins from the busy avenue that bisects his neighborhood. News that Mark had nearly been struck by a car one evening prompted the second parent conference.

This time Bill appeared annoyed. Everything about him indicated that he didn't appreciate being called in to discuss his son's problems outside of school. Nancy and I did our best to avoid coming across as judgmental, but there was no getting past the defensive wall Bill had built up around himself. He repeated his claims that he tried to spend time with Mark on the weekends and, assuming an air of authority, assured us that he would rein in his son from now on.

Further evidence of tension between Sheila and Bill emerged. Neither looked at the other as they talked, and Sheila expressed increasing frustration at her husband's lack of involvement in Mark's life. Apparently the plan to get Mark, who has splendid athletic potential, onto the local Little League baseball team had fallen through because Bill had failed to complete the necessary registration steps.

Often in cases such as this one, Nancy and I would recommend family counseling, but given Bill's heightened defensiveness, I sensed this wasn't the time or place. We ended the conference with expressions of concern over Sheila and Bill's financial stress and of hopes that things would improve soon so that they both wouldn't need to work so hard. Bill softened a little and repeated his assurances that he would keep better track of Mark's whereabouts.

The next opportunity to talk with Bill and Sheila came when we got together for the annual assessment conference that we have with every student's parents. It was Sheila who raised the issue of Mark's reading. First Nancy described the phonics program she uses with beginning readers and then her earlier one-on-one sessions with Mark. She explained how he had lost interest because of his lack of success, adding that she wasn't overly concerned because Mark was only in the first grade.

Sheila asked if there was anything she and Bill could do at home to help their son with his reading. I entered the conversation, saying that often the best thing parents can do is to read aloud to their children. Make sure that the selections are exciting, and don't turn the process into a reading lesson. The important thing is that the experience be pleasurable, which accomplishes several goals. It awakens a love of reading in children, as well as a desire to become a reader. It also helps them to internalize a feeling for reading's rhythm and flow. I added that it is a good idea, if the child isn't turned off by it, for parents to move a finger under the text as they read. This encourages children to follow along with their eyes, which helps to familiarize their brains with the fluid left-to-right tracking necessary for reading. And the more they do it, the more they will focus in on and begin to recognize individual words.

Then Nancy asked Sheila and Bill if they had a particular bedtime ritual with Mark, and if reading aloud to him was a part of it. The answer on both counts, unfortunately, was "No." Apparently on most nights Mark just put himself to bed when he was tired. Here I saw an opportunity to address two problems at once. I suggested to Bill that he be the one to read to Mark at bedtime, saying that, as Mark's most significant role model, he would have the most impact. I didn't mention aloud that this shared activity would also help to improve the bond between father and son.

Bill agreed that reading to Mark at bedtime would be good idea but said that they had no good storybooks in the house and didn't have time to go out and find any. I volunteered to go through the school's collection with Mark the following morning and allow him to pick out two or three favorites to borrow and bring home.

The conference ended on a positive note, with Sheila telling us how much she appreciated the attention we were giving Mark and how much she had seen his overall attitude improve since he had begun attending our school.

The next morning I had a private story time with Mark, as promised, and when I mentioned to him the idea of his dad reading to him at bedtime, he excitedly picked out several books to take home. However, when I asked him a few days later how the bedtime reading was going, he answered desultorily that his dad had been "too busy," staring vacantly off to my right as he told me.

Mark returned the following September, and then the September after that for a third year with us. During that time Sheila and Bill had separated permanently and Sheila had moved in with another man in a neighboring town.

Mark was given the option of whom to live with and chose his dad. In the meantime, Mark had struck up friendships with several boys who lived near the school. As he had done previously with Bert, Mark spent a lot of time at the boys' houses and frequently slept over. Word began filtering back to school from the parents of the boys that Mark's plans for returning home again were always vague or nonexistent when he was staying with them, and that they never seemed to be able to reach Bill in order to find out what his wishes were.

Reluctantly, Nancy and I decided we'd better check in with Bill about how things were going with Mark. It proved to be a mistake, though I doubt the situation would have turned out any better had we turned the matter over to the child protection agency. Bill immediately became more defensive than ever. He got openly angry for the first time, saying that he was sick and tired of our prying into his personal affairs. Finally, he told us he was putting Mark back in public school. The only concession I could win from him before he stormed out was to allow Mark to finish the week at our school so that he could have time to gather himself and make his farewells.

On Thursday I telephoned Bill at work to see if he had softened his position. His passivity had returned, but clearly he was not about to change his mind, and there was nothing I could do about it.

But Mark had an idea. On Friday he came over to the teachers' lunch table and announced that he had a plan. Apparently his dad had conceded to him that if things did not go well for Mark in public school, his father would allow him to return here. "So I'm gonna act real bad," Mark told us all, "and get them to kick me out."

Mark, carrying out his mission like a military operation, was back within three months. The last straw, we later learned, was when he hurled a string of expletives at his teacher one afternoon and she phoned Bill to tell him to come for his son immediately.

Thankfully, soon after Mark returned to the Free School he asked his mother if he could move in with her and her new partner. Sheila works in a downtown office not far from the school, so she can bring Mark in with her in the mornings. Mark's visits with his neighborhood pals now took place at clearly arranged times.

This year, his fourth with us, Mark, an unusually handsome boy with a silky brown complexion and a compact muscular build, is in the latter stages of an astounding character transformation. The vacant look is largely a relic of the past, and he has become impeccably honest in both word and deed. Now when he is animated, which is often, his eyes widen and his bushy black eyebrows raise up like Groucho Marx's.

Best of all, the fog that had settled into his mind has started to lift. At what many would consider the late age of ten, he is learning to read successfully—at his own urging. Whenever Nancy is late for his reading lesson because of pressing school business—here the administrators are also full-time teachers—he often can be seen tracking her down to ask her to please hurry up. He is learning to write, too, but because the process is still a bit cumbersome for him, he usually asks others to scribe the long, imaginative tales he likes to spin.

I might add that Mark is also teaching himself to read. Currently, he is part of a large group of kids who are enthralled with the interactive game known as Magic. The game involves reading the information contained on large sets of cards, and Mark is working very hard to catch up to the reading level of his peers so that he can be on an equal footing with them.

When someone expresses concern about our allowing kids like Mark, and a girl whom you will meet in the next chapter named Gabrielle, to put off mastering their basic skills until well into middle childhood, I usually tell them about my friend John Scott. John attended a community-like school very similar to ours in New Jersey in the 1940s called the Modern School. Free to learn when and where he pleased, John preferred to be outdoors regardless of the weather and spent many of his days tramping about in the stream that ran through the community's property.

Today John holds two Ph.D.s. He recently stepped down as chair of the department of atmospheric science at the state university here in Albany but decided he wasn't quite done with teaching. Rather than slide into a quiet retirement filled with the naturalistic pursuits that have fed his soul throughout his life, John has gone on to cofound an innovative program for undergraduates. Remembering the holistic learning of his childhood, he is attempting to break down the barriers between academic disciplines and in so doing help repair the fractured worldview with which so many young people enter college today.

The key piece of John's story, which I have intentionally saved for the end: He didn't learn to read until he was eleven.

6

So far I've presented only the stories of boys. This isn't incidental, because out of the nearly one thousand children who have passed through the Free School's doors over the years, I can probably count the number of girls who fit the typical ADHD profile on two hands. Our experience is consistent with the estimates of most reports on the issue of labeling and drugging, which show that at least 75 percent of the children in question are boys.

This year we have only one "Ritalin girl." Tanya has been with us since the age of two and a half. She is a strikingly pretty girl with a soft olive complexion and large, captivating brown eyes. Sturdily built, she greets the world with a stance that says she expects to be met on *her* terms.

Tanya's mother, Marta, was only sixteen when she gave birth to her. Marta's relationship with Tanya's father was short-lived, and Marta struggled desperately to cope with life as a single teenage mother until she met her present partner. Lamar, two years Marta's senior, is a Free School graduate—which is how Tanya came to be with us.

When she first arrived, Tanya was impulsive, aggressive, defiant, sneaky, loud, domineering, and very used to having her own way. She frequently scratched and bit other children, meaning that it was necessary to keep close tabs on her at all times. At the absolute low point, the preschool teachers had to tape cotton gloves on Tanya's hands so that she couldn't injure her playmates with her fingernails—after warning Tanya several times what the consequence would be if she didn't stop scratching. This radical, but also very pragmatic, response quickly persuaded Tanya to give up that particularly antisocial form of behavior, and it hasn't been a problem since.

Tanya's attention span was also quite brief. She would move impulsively from one activity—drawing, painting, doing puzzles, playing with toys, climbing on the jungle gym—to another, and her ability to concentrate came only in brief spurts. She rarely would sit still long enough to listen to an entire story.

Tanya, now five, has come a long way. These days she plays peacefully with the other little girls for hours on end. She still strikes out occasionally, but seldom unprovoked anymore. Those protective gloves have long since faded into memory. Instead, Tanya is generally amenable to talking through her conflicts with her peers. Her choice of language leaves a bit to be desired, but right now the preschool teachers are more interested in helping her learn to throw any kind of verbal jab rather than a physical one. Fine-tuning her wording will have to wait.

Recently, Tanya began choosing to attend Missy's kindergarten class. This is a sure sign that she is becoming sufficiently cooperative to engage in group projects and games. Missy says that Tanya's attention span has lengthened considerably and that, in fact, she is one of the brightest kids in the group. Now she enjoys being read to and is beginning to recognize and read words from her favorite stories.

An essential factor in Tanya's progress, I think, has been Marta and Lamar's willingness to let the school play a supportive role for the family as a whole. Because Lamar spent his formative years in our school, he trusts us implicitly, and he has passed that trust on to his partner. We somehow have been able to do the delicate dance of suggesting things that this young couple might do differently at home in the way of setting limits for Tanya, without causing them to feel like bad parents. We asked Marta to stop spanking Tanya and threatening her and cursing at her when she's fed up with her child's insistent antics. Conversely, we encouraged Marta not to give in to Tanya if she can possibly help it, but instead to establish consistent, non-physical consequences like sending Tanya to her room when she is disobedient or disrespectful. We also helped Lamar to find constructive ways to intervene when mother and daughter become mired in a futile battle of wills. Finally, we encouraged Marta and Lamar to take time off together. Lamar's mother lives nearby and often is willing to provide the childcare so that they can go out dancing or to the movies.

Physically and emotionally abused by both of her parents—and then by subsequent foster parents—Marta must face the role of mothering without any good models to guide her. To make matters worse, she was in many ways still a child herself when her daughter was born. Much of what we have witnessed Tanya acting out in school has been her mother's fear, her mother's frustration, her mother's rage and grief at never having received the nurturing she needed when she was growing up. Thanks to our, and much more so, Lamar's, love and support, Marta has managed to pull herself successfully into adulthood. She was able to return to high school to receive her diploma and now has a decent full-time job. Along the way, she and Lamar brought Tanya's little brother into the world, and today the four of them are busy growing strong roots together.

The Free School did not by any stretch of the imagination rescue this vulnerable young family. They rescued themselves, with some guidance from us and the help of friends and extended family. Given the sad state of disrepair into which the family in America has fallen, what they have accomplished is nothing short of heroic.

As Marta has gotten her own feet firmly underneath her, Tanya has been able to do the same—mother and daughter mirroring each other. Though the birth of a sibling rival threw her into a tailspin, Tanya quickly regained her balance and is now a loving big sister to her little brother, who is very much a male version of her.

Before Tanya, a fierce and willful fireball named Mumasatou showed up at our doors one day. I chronicled her adventures at some length in my previous book about the Free School, *Making It Up As We Go Along*.[1] The third youngest of ten brothers and sisters in a single-mother-run family, Mumasatou was with us from the age of three and a half until she entered public school for the first grade.

Mumasatou's mother, struggling to get by on public assistance, was often short-tempered and impatient. She didn't hesitate to admit that she had had her fill of taking care of children. Thus, Mumasatou was being raised as much by her older siblings, who were abusive at times, as she was by her mother. The end result was a wild, spirited little girl who was beguiling, demanding, aggressive, and sometimes violent, and always desperately hungry for attention. Whether it was positive or negative attention was of little concern to Mumasatou as she quickly shredded into tatters our usual approaches to working with young children.

To make matters even worse, Mumasatou had spent the first three years of her life in the infamous housing projects of Brooklyn's war-torn Fort Green section, where shootings were a daily occurrence. The experience left her deeply traumatized. Whenever she bumped her head, even slightly, she would grab it with both hands and begin screaming, "I'm bleeding! I'm bleeding!"

Despite my many objections to labeling children, I might have been persuaded in Mumasatou's case to go along with classifying her as suffering from posttraumatic stress disorder (PTSD), a label implying that the causes of the distress lie outside of the individual. PTSD was first associated with returning Vietnam War veterans whose psyches were overwhelmed by the constant terror of jungle warfare. Certain observers have suggested that many children growing up in urban jungles like Fort Green are being affected in ways very similar to Vietnam vets.

The move to Albany helped relieve Mumasatou's stress but by no means eliminated it. Her new neighborhood was hardly trouble-free. The family could frequently be found embroiled in one kind of crisis or another. It wasn't unusual for Mumasatou to come in with a story—always true—about a brother's arrest for selling drugs or a sister's being stabbed by a jealous boyfriend.

At the height of Mumasatou's troubled beginnings with us, when she was attacking everyone and everything in sight, we responded not with the usual forms of preschool limit setting, but instead by maintaining constant physical contact with her. For several months we either sat her in our laps or carried her from place to place like an infant. We petted and stroked her, and we took turns rocking with her in one of the three rocking chairs upstairs. If our old tricks didn't work on the days she was particularly out of sorts, then our creativity was tested until we came up with new ones.

We never for a moment considered Mumasatou to be defective or deficient. We didn't blame her for being so maddeningly

difficult at times. Instead, we began to see her repertoire of trying behaviors as a sort of code language, her only way of telling
us where it hurt and why. We assumed it to be our responsibility as her professional caregivers to break the code—not her
spirit.

Mumasatou thrived on the plentiful supply of nurturing
from teachers, interns, and older students. She soaked up the
loving touches and wasn't shy about seeking out more. Gradually, our wild child grew calmer and less aggressive. She began to
show an interest in connecting amicably with her peers. Her tolerance for frustration grew by leaps and bounds. If she began to
lose her temper while she was off playing, we invariably found
that the best response was to gather her back up again and cra-
dle and stroke her some more.

Our ability to set firm limits, along with our willingness to
respect her autonomy, set Mumasatou free to explore herself
and the world around her. In the process, she slowly shed her
insistence that she always be the center of attention and began
to develop real friendships with some of the other little girls, the
ones who refused to be dominated by her willfulness. She
largely left behind her tendency toward violent outbursts, and,
much to our relief, after six months we no longer had to moni-
tor her constantly.

The issue of girls and ADHD is an interesting one. Recent
ADHD literature, which appears to be growing increasingly
defensive as more and more people question the labeling and
drugging of millions of American children, claims that the
boy/girl ratio is equalizing. I have yet to find reliable statistics to
back up this claim.

It's not hard to understand the ADHD believers wanting the

boy/girl ratio to be more equal. The notion of gender-based neuropathology is tough to defend rationally, and science is, after all, supposed to be rational.

Common sense tells us why the majority of kids being labeled would be boys—provided, of course, that environmental factors haven't been excluded from the analysis. For starters, elementary school teachers are mainly women, and our society's track record for raising young males with a proper regard for female authority is spotty at best. In spite of all the gains of the feminist movement, the denigration of the feminine in popular culture is probably worse today than ever before. Just browse through the T-shirt collection in a low-end beachwear shop at any seaside resort. Or peruse the pornography section of your local newsstand, or surf the sex sites on the Internet.

Then consider the anger—usually unconscious—of females toward a male world that continues to disparage and demean them. Every rowdy, inattentive, overactive, mouthy, stubborn, defiant, disrespectful first or second grade boy is a glaring symbol of an eon of male oppression. Is it any wonder that there might occur a breakdown in the relationship between adult female teachers and young male students?

There are also basic differences in the makeup of the young male and female psyche that have a significant bearing on who fits into classroom routine and who doesn't. A now classic study of elementary-age schoolchildren conducted by the Fels Institute found that young girls learn primarily in response to the approval of their teachers. Boys, on the other hand, are motivated principally by the results of their own performance. Moreover, the approval of the other boys is far more important to them than the teacher's. I have observed this same phenomenon even in nonclassroom contexts such as gymnastics, in which the activity the teacher is leading is one that suits the boys' basic natures and is something *they* want to be doing. So you can imagine how this fundamental difference in the learning styles of the two genders might play itself out in situations in which the tasks are enforced and undesirable. It helps to explain why so many boys would be the ones climbing the walls in modern American classrooms, which have been stripped of almost all physicality.

A friend of mine recently suggested that girls have a kind of "psychic Ritalin" built into their systems. Girls, as the Fels study suggested, have a tendency to internalize automatically the control of the teacher—there's no need for chemical reinforcement. Meanwhile, the dynamics of the conventional classroom, like those of the military or the modern corporation, require that students surrender their own wills, inclinations, and internal rhythms. The end result: increasing numbers of children, especially boys, who elect to challenge the system in the only way they know how, with aberrant behavior and the refusal to pay attention, cooperate, or perform.

For argument's sake, let's assume the ADHD believers are correct, that the number of girls being labeled with ADHD is rising substantially. Does this assumption lend proof to their theory that ADHD is an organic brain disorder? Actually, when you think about it, there are several environmental factors that might explain why the number of girls being labeled might be growing, too.

Two very powerful forces, neither of which has much to do with gender, have been coming to the fore of late. On the one hand, there is the ever-increasing pressure on schools to raise academic standards, and on the other there is an increasing absence of adult authority in our culture. Robert Bly describes this phenomenon in his book *Sibling Society,* stating that, due to numerous upheavals in the values of the culture over the past several generations, no one really grows up anymore.[2] This, of course, means there isn't anybody left to play the role of a true parent—hence the book's title. The lack of effective parenting today, writes Bly, is leaving children confused about issues of authority, and it is placing entirely too much power in their young hands. Thus, the task of controlling the behavior of a roomful of increasingly willful students is becoming an almost hopeless one, despite all of the recent training emphasis on so-called classroom management.

And then, according to James Garbarino in *Raising Children in a Socially Toxic Environment*, there is the increasing "social toxicity" of American culture. By this Garbarino means "the idea that the mere act of living in our society is now dangerous to the health and well-being of children and adolescents . . . whose personality, temperament, and life experiences make them especially vulnerable."[3] While girls may be both genetically and temperamentally more resilient than boys to what Garbarino calls the "rising nastiness" in American culture, they are by no means immune. So why wouldn't we begin to see young girls as well as boys showing signs of rising distress both at home and in school?

Mumasatou's progress during her second year with us was dramatic. She became the school's unofficial ambassador, greeting first-time visitors with a big hug and then showing them around the upstairs. She alternated between group play and more private pursuits depending on her mood. Slowly but surely she gained control over her impulses.

Around the time she turned five, Mumasatou began following the other little girls into Missy's kindergarten class. She was curious to see what went on behind the only other closed door in the preschool besides the bathroom, but reluctant to join in on the project the kids and Missy were working on together. Missy's working arrangement with Mumasatou was as follows: As long as Mumasatou didn't disturb the others, she was welcome to remain in the room. Missy provided plenty of alternative things for Mumasatou to do, puzzles, drawing materials, quiet games, and storybooks, so that she could amuse herself if that was what she preferred.

Missy, meanwhile, was always encouraging and enticing Mumasatou to join in on the fun—and the way Missy teaches kindergarten it is nothing but fun. Sometimes Missy would succeed, but she soon discovered that it was still difficult for Mumasatou to share Missy's attention with five or six other rivals. So, Missy began asking one of the college interns to assist her, which seemed to relieve some of the pressure. On her good days, Mumasatou would participate in the activities Missy had planned for the day. On her so-so days she would alternate between the shared activity and her own individual pursuits, and on her bad days, she would disrupt the class until Missy had to ask her to go out in the big room and play. Missy was careful never to get angry with Mumasatou at such moments. She would always thank Mumasatou for coming in and then remind her that she was welcome back the next day.

On her very bad days, when Mumasatou arrived at school ready to burst, she seemed to have an instinct not even to try kindergarten, and instead she would spend the morning playing actively in the big room or the backyard. Often on these days she appointed herself the surrogate mother of Michel, a two-year-old French boy who was experiencing a prolonged bout of separation anxiety from his mom. Michel trusted Mumasatou implicitly and was delighted to have her read to him or push him around the big room in a makeshift carriage or on the swing set in the yard. When Michel was upset, he would go to Mumasatou as readily as he would to Missy or the other preschool teachers.

Missy, Nancy, and I all felt that, all things considered, Mumasatou was making excellent progress. But toward the end of the school year, Mumasatou began making noises about going to another school. Whenever she was especially upset over not getting her way, her favorite expression of protest became, "I hate this *stupid* school. Next year I'm going to Giffen." Giffen is the elementary school four blocks from her house, which several of her siblings attended.

We didn't think Mumasatou was at all ready for public school, and we advised her mother on more than one occasion that Mumasatou might not be able to cope with the loss of individuality and lack of attention in a class with twenty-five to thirty other kids and only one adult.

The response usually went something like, "I just don't know what I'm going to do with that little girl. She's always got some crazy idea in her head."

But leave us she did. Without any notice, Mumasatou's mother enrolled her in Giffen the following September. Things apparently did not go well from the outset. Within days we began hearing reports that Mumasatou wasn't fitting in. Finally, when her exasperated and, no doubt, overwhelmed teacher sent her packing to the principal's office one morning, Mumasatou ran right out of the building, not to be intercepted until she had already crossed the busy avenue on which the school stands. Rumor has it that this same scenario repeated itself several times, until Mumasatou was taken to the district office for "testing."

Within a month I learned from Mumasatou's mother that Mumasatou had been labeled with ADHD and assigned to a suburban school for "emotionally disturbed" children, where she was being administered Ritalin and another drug, the name of which her mother couldn't pronounce. Leave it to Mumasatou to have set the Albany School District's all-time record for the shortest stay in a regular classroom.

I have no quarrels with the school system's determination that Mumasatou was "emotionally disturbed," because to a certain extent she was. It's just that I dreaded the thought of that proud, feisty, creative, intelligent, courageous, caring young person being drugged as though she were some sort of runaway rhino.

But I would be the last one to blame Mumasatou's neighborhood school for being unable to handle her. Even we, with all of our extra human resources and flexible structure, were stretched to our outer limits. There was no way that that beleaguered and outnumbered first grade teacher was going to be able to redress the effects of the violent, chaotic world into which Mumasatou was born. There was no way she could replace Mumasatou's deficit of positive, nurturing attention, no way she could repair Mumasatou's damaged sense of self quickly enough for Mumasatou to be able to manage in her classroom.

Mumasatou is a classic example of the child who has experienced too many adversity factors. In one such study, researchers found that it is the accumulation of "adversity indicators" in a child's life—poverty, father absence, minority group status, low parental education, parental substance abuse, dysfunctional child-rearing styles, large family size, parental mental illness—that jeopardizes a child's mental and emotional development.[4] Most children are resilient enough to cope with one or two strikes against them, but kids with three or more begin to suffer significant declines.

Another study, this one conducted by Harvard Medical School's Joseph Biederman, M.D., confirms the same findings.[5] After investigating the backgrounds of 260 kids for evidence of the abovementioned adversity indicators, he found that the odds of a child being diagnosed with ADHD were 7.4 times greater if he or she had one adversity indicator, 9.5 times greater for two, 34.6 times great for three, and 41.7 times greater if the child had four indicators.

Another reason I think Mumasatou was unable to cope in public school was that she suddenly found herself in an environment devoid of human touch. In *Touching: The Human Significance of the Skin*, Ashley Montagu addressed the critical role touch plays in a child's healthy cognitive and emotional growth. Referring to touch as the "mother of the senses," he noted that it is the human embryo's first sensory experience. Moreover, he said, the skin arises from the same basic cell layer as the nervous system—hence his use of the phrase "the mind of the skin" to emphasize the intimate connection between the two.

Montagu's extensive research in human anatomy, biology, and anthropology led him to conclude that normal development in children cannot occur unless they receive enough touching and affection. "The infant's need for body contact is compelling. If that need is not adequately satisfied, even though all other needs are met, it will suffer."[6]

Montagu pointed out numerous studies showing that institutionalized infants who were seldom handled by their caregivers showed serious signs of mental and social retardation. Conversely, he discussed at great length the child-rearing practices of several indigenous cultures, the foundation of which is the constant skin-to-skin contact between mother and infant— for no less than the first year of life. Again and again researchers confirmed that children raised in this way were far superior developmentally to the average child in the industrialized West. More recently, Jean Liedloff, who spent several years living with a Stone Age indigenous people in South America, reached the very same conclusion in her book *The Continuum Concept*.

Montagu also referred to case studies of older children and adults whose psychic damage was repaired by massive amounts of tactile stimulation. Such was our instinctive response to Mumasatou's antisocial behavior, which we took as a signal that she needed our special attention and not as evidence that she had a neurologically based behavioral "disorder." Her starting to get better as soon as we provided it only confirmed our interpretation.

It's no mystery why Mumasatou had never gotten the touching and affection she needed. Her mother, nearly forty by the time she was born, was overwhelmed by the demands of single parenting. Whenever I had the occasion to be in Mumasatou's home, I would find her infant brother plopped in his playpen in front of the TV—the babysitter without arms. And in an apartment crowded with rival siblings all hungry for attention, most of the touches Mumasatou received were anything but loving ones.

At school, however, she quickly began to make up for the deficiency. Could another reason that so many more boys than girls are exhibiting symptoms of distress be that girls are far more likely to seek out being touched and held? I know of no research that addresses this question; however, all of my experience with children tells me it is true. A great many of the boys that I have worked with over the years were to one degree or another resistant to receiving affection, an indication to me that they had been deprived of it in early childhood.

In general, no one gets touched enough in modern American culture. According to Marianna Caplin in *Untouched*, we are an "untouched nation," and our touch-starved children are paying an especially heavy price.[7] Two-thirds of all mothers with preschool-age kids are working mothers. The vast majority of them place their infants in institutional day care, where there are strict policies about physical contact with children. Unfortunately, the ever-increasing reports of touch crimes against children have taken their toll, forcing schools and day-care centers everywhere to insist that teachers keep their professional distance. Fortunately, we at the Free School are bound by no such prohibitions.

So, no, I don't blame Giffen School for being unable to give Mumasatou what she needed. If there is fault to be found, it is with a society that does precious little to support its children and that elects to tranquilize them rather than create a more tranquil world for them to grow up in.

Reaching back nearly two decades into our school's history, we find Gabrielle, another member of our select group of Ritalin girls. Gabrielle, or Gaby, as she preferred to be called, spent her entire childhood with us. Her parents enrolled her in the preschool when she was only two, and she remained until she graduated from the eighth grade.

Long-legged and lithe with bright blue eyes and a head full of wispy blond curls, Gaby was a gentle, playful, extremely imaginative little girl. Her parents, who operated a law partnership out of their home in the neighborhood, were strong supporters of the Free School's approach to education, and in fact moved into the neighborhood in order to be closer to the school. They would later enroll their second child, Tim, who also stayed with us through eighth grade.

What I remember most about Gaby as a young child is how happy and carefree she was. She loved to do all the things that little girls like to do, dress up as mommies and play with baby dolls, sing and dance, listen to long stories—her father was an excellent storyteller—and most of all to draw. Gaby loved drawing more than anything else. Her artistic output was prodigious, and her giftedness was evident even in her earliest crayon-scribble sketches and tempera paint portraits. By the time she was five she was creating unicorns exhibiting a striking level of sophistication.

To top it all off, Gaby had a soul mate with whom to share the magical world she set out to recreate every day. Desiree was a chocolaty version of Gaby, with brown curls instead of blond ones. Both started in the school at about the same time, and within months they were inseparable. Today, nearly twenty years later, they are still the best of friends—even though Desi moved away when they were seven and their lives since have taken very different turns.

When Gaby and Desi entered Rosalie's first grade class downstairs, drawing and painting the make-believe realm of dragons and princesses that they shared continued to be their primary passion. And when they weren't busy fashioning representations of their dream world they were busy dressing up and acting it out. Gaby and Desi's relationship wasn't an exclusive one by any means. Others were welcome to join in if they wanted to. It was just that they didn't need anyone else to make their universe complete. Their fertile imaginations supplied all of the necessary energy.

Part of this story is about what quite different individuals Gaby and Desi were. For instance, Desi wasn't nearly the artist that Gaby was. Desi was always happy to draw and paint alongside her best friend, but she had a dancer's body and preferred to do physical things like dance and wrestle and jump rope. She also liked nothing better than to tease the boys and get them going.

Another dissimilarity showed itself in the classroom: While Desi was quick to develop reading, writing, and math skills, Gaby was not. The difference here, I think, lay in the orientation of their brains. In Desi's case, the left side of her brain, the side responsible for sequential-thinking tasks such as the three "R's," was dominant. The opposite was true in Gaby's case. For her, the right side of her brain, the side where images are formed, was far more active than the left. This is an altogether common scenario for highly artistic children like Gaby. Gaby was able to pick up phonics readily enough because Rosalie employed a fun, right-brained method based on colorful images and rhymes that continually engages the imagination. But when it came to the linear task of stringing the symbols together into words and sentences, Gaby lost interest and got out her sketchpad and markers instead. The same was true with arithmetic. The concepts didn't come easily to her, and even when she did catch on to some of them, she found little satisfaction in her accomplishment. For her, math was simply boring and that was that.

At the same time, Gaby continued to love being read to. Her parents did so religiously at bedtime, and we read to her every day in school. By the time she was eight she had listened to the entire J. R. R. Tolkien series. Gaby also loved to write poetry, although she would dictate her work to others because she found the writing process too tedious and cumbersome. She was such a good poet that at one point she won first prize in a poetry contest sponsored by the Albany Public Library, in which a substantial number of area schools participated.

Gaby's creativity continued to blossom as she grew older. However, her left-brained academic skills for the most part lay dormant. When she reached the age of nine and still wasn't reading, her family began to grow concerned. Her mother and father weren't overly worried because they trusted in their daughter's intelligence and believed in the school's relaxed philosophy of learning. It helped, too, that we teachers had been reassuring them from time to time that when Gaby decided to set her mind to learning to read, learn she would.

But as fate would have it, Gaby's mother's mother and her father's sister were both reading specialists. The grandmother was a remedial reading expert, and the aunt had developed a reading instruction program that she taught to public school teachers. Quite understandably given their backgrounds, both women were increasingly alarmed that Gaby wasn't reading yet, and their anxiety began seeping into Gaby's household.

In order to allay everyone's fear, we invited Gaby's grandmother to come to the school and share with us some of her remedial reading teaching techniques and materials. Gaby's parents somewhat reluctantly consulted with Gaby about the possibility of her working on her reading with a tutor an afternoon or two a week after school. Gaby, who appeared largely oblivious to the drama that was kicking up around her, agreed to try it out. She also began working with some of her grandma's reading materials at school.

Thankfully, Gaby liked her tutor very much and thoroughly enjoyed their private, one-on-one sessions. Within months she was reading with ease. The interesting thing was that—and I have observed the same phenomenon in other so-called late readers—as soon as Gaby had sufficiently broken the code, she began reading sophisticated literature. Also, Gaby could frequently be found with a good book in her hands. Reading never replaced art as her first love, but it did become a close second. She was very pleased to now have the ability to read to herself.

And then in turn, as Gaby's reading experience increased, her writing skills began to fall into place as well. I'm not sure she ever became the world's greatest speller, but with the advent of modern word-processing technology, the importance of a broad spelling vocabulary is greatly diminished.

Math and Gaby, however, remained distant cousins. With Gaby's reading "crisis" resolved, at home there was no longer any worry about her academic progress and she was once again left free to draw, paint, sculpt, write poetry, and read magical novels to her heart's content. And so it went until Gaby began her twelfth and final year with us, when she sat down next to me one morning said, "Chris, I need to do something about my math. I'm probably going to go to Albany High next year, and I don't want to be way behind the other kids."

The earnest look on her face told me that hers was no small concern. I remember answering her with something like, "Hey, I don't think it will be a problem. If you have regular lessons with me, we'll have you caught up in no time. The things you need to learn aren't really all that hard."

When I asked when she wanted to get started, she replied, "Right now."

So we headed straight for an available chalkboard for a long session to figure out exactly what she did and didn't know. We quickly discovered that she knew a lot more than she realized, which is commonly the case in situations in which children aren't forced to digest a daily diet of basic skills work. These kids usually learn a great deal about manipulating numbers simply in the course of their daily experience.

But it was evident that it was going to take hard work and commitment on Gaby's part in order to master the K–8 math curriculum in a single year. Though she now had a much better grasp of linear thinking than she did when she was younger, she was by no means one of those lucky kids who need only to see something once in order to understand and remember it. She still didn't particularly like numbers, either. Her only real motivation was that she wanted to be prepared for ninth grade.

I decided to start Gaby out with long multiplication. First I snuck in a quick review of the concept of place value using manipulatable blocks that are particularly helpful to right-brained learners because they can see and feel the structural concept of ones, tens, hundreds, and so on. She caught on quickly. But when it came time to tackle the pattern of multiplying and then adding the rows of numbers together, she grew frustrated. If Gaby had been younger and we had had more time, I would have gotten out the Cuisenaire rods and other hands-on materials to help her visualize the basis for the pattern. But Gaby was going to have to learn math by standard methods the next year, so I decided it would be better to proceed using those now.

I did stop so that we could explore her trouble. I explained to her how her brain just wasn't organized in such a way as to easily recognize linear patterns, and that this was common in people with a lot of artistic talent. I reassured her that she was perfectly capable of internalizing the patterns—it would just take a little more practice.

I also did a couple of things to reduce the degree of difficulty. I had Gaby postpone learning her multiplication tables—which can be an arduous task for some—and instead provided her with a "magic square" that contained all the facts on a single piece of cardboard. I also started her out working large on the chalkboard, because bigger numbers make pattern recognition easier and the physicality helps to allay anxiety.

After a couple of days Gaby was whizzing accurately through complex problems. With her confidence mushrooming, I asked her if she felt she was ready to memorize her times tables. Was she ever. To my absolute amazement, it took her less than a week to nail them down tight.

Long division was next. Again we began on the chalkboard because the pattern, with its alternating steps of division, multiplication, subtraction, bringing down a new number, and then dividing again, can be daunting at first. Again I was amazed at how fast Gaby caught on. I think she was even on the verge of declaring math fun because it was becoming so easy.

So that Gaby wouldn't be dependent on me, and so that she could work on her math whenever she wanted to, I introduced her to the set of self-teaching workbooks that I'm fond of using because they are adequately self-explanatory and contain the answers so that kids can check their own work. She began plowing through them with great determination, frequently taking them home so that she could do them in the evenings and on weekends.

It took Gaby only a few months to complete the whole eight-book series, which she did largely on her own with occasional help from me. Then we went back to regular sessions together so that she could learn enough geometry and algebra to get ready for high school. Gaby found no particular pleasure in the work. Her desire to be prepared for ninth grade was sufficient motivation to keep her on track.

Imagine how different the picture might have been had fate landed Gaby in a conventional school instead of in ours. She might have slipped through without being tagged with ADHD or some such, because fifteen years ago kids weren't labeled and drugged nearly as routinely as they are today. But her teachers almost certainly would have determined that she had a learning problem, and she very likely would have been funneled into one kind of remedial program or another. The end result in terms of

Gaby's academic achievement might well have been the same, but at what cost to her soul and spirit?

Far many more times than I can count I have listened to depressing stories told by parents who unwittingly placed their children in school environments that were ill suited to their kids' personalities, temperaments, and learning styles. I often grow angry when I hear how the parents watched with growing alarm as their formerly cheerful, curious, and engaging children began to turn away from life and withdraw inward. My anger isn't toward the parents, or even the schools. It is toward a nation that appears to be oblivious to the human wreckage caused by what education author Susan Ohanian calls "one-size-fits-all schooling."

Gaby's final day at the Free School was triumphant. Not only was she prepared to move on to the next step in her education, but she was about to be the unquestioned star of the big talent show that always follows our graduation ceremony. Gaby had prepared a skit that to this day remains one of the funniest children's theater productions I have ever seen. She called it "TV Sucks Your Brains Out," an obvious loving poke at her parents, who had put away the family television years before because they didn't like the effect it was having on their kids.

The skit went something like this: Two children lived in a home where there was a TV in the closet they weren't allowed to watch. One Sunday afternoon, the kids' father tricked them into going outside so that he could sneak the television out to watch a little football. The kids quickly caught on, however, and somehow managed to trick their dad in return so that they could get in a little TV watching of their own.

Unbeknownst to the audience, the two siblings had clear

plastic bags filled with cooked spaghetti hidden under their hats while they were sitting in front of the television set that Gaby had cleverly constructed out of cardboard. Each bag had a strand of invisible monofilament fishing line attached to it that then ran along the floor and into the hands of an accomplice hiding behind the TV screen. All of a sudden, after the kids had been staring at the set for a while, the accomplice yanked the kids' "brains" out from under their caps and slowly dragged them across the stage and into the hungry mouth of the TV. It was an ingenious sight gag. People were laughing so hard that some literally fell out of their seats, and it took several minutes to restore enough order to bring on the next act.

Despite Gaby's steadfast preparations, her transition into a large, centralized public high school was not easy in the beginning. The almost exclusive regimen of textbook-based, left-brained academic work presented a real challenge. For the first few weeks, it took her several hours to complete all her homework to her satisfaction. Her initial quiz and test scores were low, but above the passing mark. Determined to succeed, Gaby applied herself with such persistence that by the end of the first grading period her name could be found on the honor roll— where it would remain throughout her high school career.

Along the way, Gaby became friends with the head of the school's art department, who recognized Gaby's gift and, within the narrow confines of the curriculum, helped to further nourish it. Their relationship also helped Gaby to endure a school day that for her was nothing short of tedious. The teacher would later be an honored guest at Gaby's graduation party.

As I write this, Gaby is just beginning her senior year at a well-known private college with an excellent reputation for the arts. There she has continued to experiment in several different media, and last year she had her first, very successful, one-woman show. She also discovered a passion for a new medium, playwriting, which eventually became her major.

Where Gaby's life will lead her after she finishes college is anybody's guess. But I think we can all rest assured that it will be interesting.

The moral of the stories of our three "Ritalin girls" is this: While neither Tanya, Mumasatou, nor Gaby conformed to the current behavioral and/or academic norms that we as a society have set down for schoolchildren, none of them was suffering from a brain-based neurological disorder. They didn't need daily doses of Ritalin—classified in Europe as a performance drug just like steroids and other performance-enhancing substances that athletes are prone to misusing—to help them learn and behave acceptably. What they needed—and received—was a school environment that loved and nurtured them, offered support to their families, and, above all, made room for their abundant uniqueness.

7

December greets us with an early, heavy snowfall. The afternoon following the storm is sunny and calm, and with temperatures hovering right around the freezing point the conditions are perfect for sledding. The entire downstairs group bundles up excitedly for the fifteen-minute slog to Lincoln Park, home of Albany's best sledding spot, also known as Dead Man's Hill. Some of the kids have come in prepared with shiny polyester snowsuits, while others make do by doubling up with extra pairs of pants from the school's winter clothing box.

Sledding is a major winter event at the Free School. A tangible anticipation always propels the first outing. While Dave and the older kids are breaking out the school's ragtag collection of sleds, coasters, and saucers—mostly plastic—I dash home to fetch my wife's Flexible Flyer, a venerable oaken treasure preserved from her childhood. I like it because it can be steered, and also because three or four kids can pile onto it together for an often unforgettable ride down the steep slope.

When William sees the old sled, he is instantly enamored of it. He rushes to my side, yelling out, "Can I have this one, Chris? Can I? Can I? PLEASE!"

You might expect William to have a battle on his hands for such a prize, but the kids who were in the school last year know how much work it is to drag the heavy sled all the way to the park and up the long incline. So no one else steps forward to compete for it. Before I hand over the pull rope to William, I advise him, "It will be really hard work to pull this sled all the way to the park, especially up Dead Man's Hill."

"That's okay; I can do it," he replies nonchalantly.

William steadfastly brings up the rear on our trek through the deep snow, twice refusing my offer to help him out with the sled. Born in New York City, he has never been sledding before and seems driven to prove something—to himself and the rest of the world.

All goes well until we near our final destination. I glance back only to see that William is no longer following the scraggly line of kids who are taking the longer but much easier route to the top, along the sideways spine of the hill. Clearly, William has already drawn a mental straight line between him and the summit and has set his course accordingly.

I wait for William to experience the absurd degree of difficulty he has chosen for himself before I say anything. When he falls flat on his face for the third time I shout back, "Hey, William, this way is much less slippery. I promise you'll get there faster if you follow us."

William responds with a look of fierce determination. He manages to regain his footing, but as soon as he tries to take another step upward, he falls again. This time he hits the snow so awkwardly that he loses his grip on the pull rope, allowing the heavy sled to slide riderless back to the bottom and erasing his hard-won ten yards of progress. As he stumbles down to retrieve the sled, I turn to catch up with the others, assuming that William has gotten the message and will take the easy way up now.

After several minutes of standing at the top with Dave, the two of us sharing our amusement over the kids' wide variety of sledding styles, I realize that William still hasn't appeared. I walk to where I can peek down over the ridge and can hardly believe my eyes. There he is, right back on the same crazy trajectory, only slightly farther up the hill than he was before. Sledless again, he is entirely bootless now, too, trying to crawl up on all fours. Thick tears are streaming down his once proud face. It's time for a rescue.

I slide quickly down on my backside to help William put himself back together. I retrieve his boots, which have been sucked off by the soft, spongy snow, and put them back on over his wet socks. Suppressing a smile, I ask him if he'd like me to bring the sled to the top of the hill. This time he answers with a snuffled "Yes." Without further words we skid back down together, gather up the sled, and head to our left to pick up the trail the rest of the group has trampled on this otherwise unblemished hillside.

William has just encountered a natural force into which his willfulness could scarcely put a dent, and he is profoundly moved.

By the time we reach the top, William's tears have dried, leaving faint tracks on his rosy brown complexion. He asks me quietly for the sled, heads straight for the edge, and places the sled upside down in the snow. He must think the runners are handrails. He mounts the sled eagerly, but when nothing happens in spite of his scooting, he shoots a quizzical look back at Dave and me.

"Turn the sled over," I call out.

He follows my instructions, except that now he has the sled backwards. One of the other boys tries to point out his mistake, but William ignores him and gets back on anyway. Not wanting to see him wipe out on the very first ride of his life, I rush over before he can kick himself loose, explaining to him that the wooden crossbar is the front of the sled and can be used to steer it from side to side.

Perhaps instinctively, William has chosen a spot on the slope that isn't so precipitous. I suggest to him that he lie down on the sled, but he is determined to go down in a sitting position like the rest of the kids. I give the sled a gentle nudge to get it going, and off he shoots like a broncobuster, feet thrashing the air, both hands locked in a death grip on the pull rope. Thanks only to a marvelous sense of balance, he makes it all the way to the bottom and glides to a stop with a victory whoop. Dave and I applaud and shout our congratulations from the top.

Faced with another ascent of the hill, William again begins a frontal assault on the steepest section. My only response to his pleas for help is to point toward the diagonal routes the other kids are taking. Finally, after five more minutes of futile struggle, he changes course and reaches the crest for the second time. He is grinning from ear to ear and ready for more.

Several of William's classmates immediately clamor around to ask if they can join him for the next ride. William is in such a state of elation that he agrees without hesitation. Dave and I help to arrange the compact, excited bodies on the sled, showing the kids how to interlock their boots around the rider in front. We give them a gentle shove, and with fearless young William at the helm they hurtle downward at a very high rate of speed, screaming as though they're on a runaway roller coaster. By about mid-slope the chain of children begins to come unlinked, each kid leaning out wildly in a different direction. A small hump in the snow suddenly finishes them off, but somehow, in perfect synchrony, all four bodies slip off the sled at once, still semiattached. While the sled silently completes the trip without them, the kids' momentum snowballs them into a howling, giggling tangle of arms and legs—a perfect ending for this crew.

The four classmates happily share the job of dragging the old oak sled back up to the top. They spend the remainder of the afternoon perfecting their group technique, managing to put together several flawless rides before we all head back to school, joyful and exhausted.

Temperamental, highly charged children like William desperately need real-life challenges against which to test themselves. This is the best antidote I know of to their almost addictive tendency toward placing themselves continually in opposition to others. Let nature become the teacher. She never takes anything personally and always seems to deliver her lessons in just the right measure, at just the right time.

If William is not hounded prematurely into mastering academic tasks for which he is not yet ready, the day shall come when he will eagerly choose to tackle the mental challenges presented by reading, writing, and arithmetic. My optimistic prediction, however, depends heavily on the trust and patience of his parents and teachers. Unfortunately, William's mother and father are growing increasingly restive. We're beginning to hear frequent expressions of concern at how much time William spends in school "playing," not "working." Unfortunately, too, Nancy and I are finding ourselves running out of ways to reassure them. It certainly doesn't help that William is showing few signs of interest in his class's reading and writing projects. Because William is quick with numbers, I am occasionally able to draw him into doing a little math, which encourages his parents somewhat. Still, their primary concern continues to be his inability to read.

I have no trouble understanding Irene and William Senior's anxiety. Our society constantly bombards parents with fear messages about their children. All of the recent hype around "standards" only makes a bad situation worse in the case of families such as William's where there needs to be less pressure, not more, placed on a child to acquire left-brain academic skills at a young age. Moreover, when "Big" William isn't moving refrigerators for a living, he's driving tractor-trailers. He says he wants something better for his son, and he sees success in school as the key to prosperity.

If only we could find some way to convince William's parents of the value of his play, and how it will gradually contribute to his transformation into an able reader. Einstein was right about the imagination. It is more important than knowledge. William, through his play, is learning to imagine himself in entirely new ways. He is discovering, however haltingly, the value of belonging to a community, one to which he brings his own unique and important contribution. He now knows that when you are a member of a group, you don't always get your own way. Furthermore, he is learning how to deal with success and failure on his own terms, and how to make his own corrections when his present strategy isn't getting him where he wants to go. This is the beautiful wisdom of children's play: It weaves incentive and consequence into an internal tapestry of meaning, and in so doing performs an integral role in the unfolding of intelligence.

I have learned most of what I know about Ritalin kids from children like William who have attended our school. But occasionally I've learned important lessons from a child who merely visits our school. Paul was one such boy. He came to the school for a trial visit, but in that one brief week he taught me a great deal about the inner dynamics of the behaviors that get kids labeled and drugged. Like Damian, Paul had been diagnosed with ADHD in kindergarten. By the middle of his first grade year, his mother had grown disturbed by Ritalin's effects on him and decided to explore other alternatives.

A slender, angular boy, blond and blue-eyed, Paul had hair like fine straw. His hands always seemed to tremor slightly. His speech was about as rapid-fire as any I can remember. Conversing with him was an adventure because his mind seemed to operate at or near the speed of light. He tended to shift subjects with great rapidity, making it a challenge to keep up with him. And like most Ritalin kids when they first arrive, he was continually on the move.

Paul taught me an important lesson about ADHD while we were doing some math together one morning. I was having considerable difficulty holding his attention. His mind would chase the slightest distraction, and I was on the verge of giving up. As I went one more round with his inattentiveness, I quickly thought the problem through. It was definitely not disinterest on Paul's part. Clearly, he liked math very much; in fact, our one-on-one session had been his idea in the first place. Nor was it frustration, because he was proudly firing off correct answers with ease. It was not my inexperience, either. Over the years I have successfully shown scores of students how to perform carrying in long addition. Furthermore, he seemed to like me as a teacher.

Maybe Paul's high-speed thinking was rubbing off on me already, because an idea suddenly occurred to me. I decided to pick up my tempo in an attempt to match his, an act that involved doubling the ordinary cadence of my speech, perhaps even tripling it. I sped through the steps one more time and then raced him into a series of demonstration examples. The change in Paul was absolutely astounding. He grew as calm and focused as you could imagine a high-strung boy like him becoming. We were flying through the lesson together. But if my momentum flagged for even a moment, Paul's hands would start to quiver again—a sure sign I was about to lose him. The lesson stretched on for thirty minutes or so, by far the longest span I'd seen him spend in one place. By the time Paul proudly announced he wanted to stop, he had so thoroughly gotten the hang of carrying that he was able to add three-digit numbers with 100 percent accuracy.

After Paul had picked up his things and zoomed on to another room, I leaned back in my chair with my hands folded behind my head and let out a sigh of relief. It felt a little like I had just run a mile at a very fast pace.

Why did Paul relax when I caught up to and mentally sprinted alongside him? To this day I'm not sure; however, I can report that I have since employed the same tactic with a number of other similarly wired boys, always with the same positive results.

Thus far, the only thing I have found in the literature to provide me with any clues to this puzzling phenomenon is a book entitled *The Gift of Dyslexia,* by Ronald Davis.[1] Interestingly, the term *dyslexia* dates from the 1920s and was the first term used to refer to learning problems in school, while today it has been largely replaced by the new medicalized nomenclature. I don't have as much trouble with this childhood label because according to my *Webster's* it means simply "a disturbance in the ability to read."

Dyslexic himself, Davis says that dyslexics tend to think in images rather than in words like most people. Verbal thinking is linear, meaning that its speed is limited to about 250 words per minute, the highest possible rate at which words can be intelligibly strung together. Nonverbal thinking, on the other hand, is possibly thousands of times faster, hence the "gift" of dyslexia. Davis notes that numerous twentieth-century geniuses, among them Einstein and Edison, are thought to have been dyslexic.

The downside for image-based thinkers is that it leaves them ill equipped for reading, especially at a young age. Dyslexic children, according to Davis, have particular difficulty learning to read words that don't refer to concrete experience. Whereas they are able to create permanent memory slots for *elephant* and *run,* articles and prepositions—the connective tissue of written language—remain unintelligible and even shifting strings of gibberish. Davis has developed a highly successful method for teaching dyslexics to read, based, in part, on the reader's fashioning models and scenes out of clay depicting the abstract words that are so difficult for them to decode.

Davis's hard-won understanding of his own perceptual mechanics and his ongoing work with dyslexic kids have convinced him that dyslexia is not the result of neurological dysfunction. For reasons unexplored in the book, Davis believes that dyslexics develop their multidimensional means of perception as a way of coping with an underlying feeling of disorientation, one that is maximally aroused by the linear, sequential tasks that fill up the hours of the conventional classroom day. He says many kids diagnosed with ADHD are actually dyslexics who have been mislabeled. Their distractibility and "hyperactivity" are additional, physiological reactions to their sense of inner confusion.

The Davis version of dyslexia fit six-year-old Paul perfectly. I had also discovered during Paul's week with us that he was not yet reading. In fact, he had shown no interest whenever I invited him to read with me. On the one occasion when I gently insisted, he appeared so agitated and confused that I quickly decided to the cut the session short.

One final claim from Davis's book of particular relevance: The mental confusion suffered by dyslexic children usually subsides of its own accord around the age of eight or nine. We have observed this same tendency in children who begin reading at an age later than most, though we don't refer to them as "dyslexic," or anything else for that matter.

The trouble, of course, is that contemporary society considers it a crisis if a child isn't well on the road to literacy by the age of six or seven. At this point someone invariably pushes the panic button, and the ensuing anxiety and pressure only further complicate and confuse the learning process for the young non-reader. A "reading problem" is born.

Many of us don't realize that it wasn't always this way. As recently as the 1950s, the conventional methodology for teaching reading allowed for different children to pick up on reading at different points in childhood. A pamphlet on reading instruction from that period published by the New York State Teachers College includes a vignette featuring three hypothetical first graders. One was precocious and already reading. The second responded well to typical classroom methods. The third student, presented as a squirmy, flighty, and inattentive boy—always the first one out the door at recess time and the last to come back in—was not responding to instruction and was rapidly "falling behind" the others.

Did the pamphlet's authors diagnose the boy with some sort of disability or disorder? Quite the contrary. They took great pains to point out to young teachers in training that here was a *normal*, energetic, and active boy who was not yet ready to settle into the long stints of passive attentiveness that learning to read in a large public school classroom requires. They cautioned—rightly so—against pushing such students at this early stage of the game, warning that in so doing the teacher runs a great risk of reinforcing patterns of failure and a generalized resistance to learning. Be patient and prepared, they counseled, to wait until the third grade, when high-energy kids naturally begin to acquire the ability to concentrate on sedentary, linear mental tasks such as reading.

At the Free School, we have always found great variability in the age at which children are truly ready to read. There have been a few kids who have learned as early as four, and a few as late as nine or ten. The so-called late readers all learned to read just as well as the early ones, and then they read avidly once they mastered the process because they were never stigmatized with the false notion that they had a reading problem.

It was actually Paul's mother who provided me with one of my initial insights about the parents of the kids who get labeled with ADHD. She had stayed on for Paul's first day, along with Paul's four-year-old sister, Tina, who was visiting in the preschool. This provided us with an excellent opportunity to observe the interaction between mother and children.

Brenda was a large woman, thirty or forty pounds overweight. Dark, shoulder-length hair framed a face that looked perpetually annoyed. I was given the impression that her family had gone through a lot of upheaval in the last several years. No longer with the kids' father, Brenda informed me that enrolling her children in the Free School was dependent on their relocating to Albany from their present home in a rural trailer park about twenty-five miles away.

While Brenda was busy upstairs hovering over Tina, monitoring her every move in the dress-up corner, I quietly invited Paul downstairs to introduce him to the other first graders. We were sitting together at the big table telling Paul how the school works when Brenda bustled in and sat down at the end opposite me. I immediately noticed a shift in Paul. His attention seemed to vacate the room.

It wasn't long before his mother was in hot pursuit: "Paul, listen to your teacher."

Paul's eyes turned back toward me. I resumed my explanation of the council meeting system but sensed that he was with us only in body. He began to squirm vigorously in his seat.

Brenda went after him again. "Paul, stop your fidgeting and sit still."

Then one of his prospective classmates tried to inform Paul that we go swimming every Thursday and that he should bring in a bathing suit, towel, and twenty-five cents if he wanted to come along, but Paul was looking off in another direction again and taking little if anything in.

"Paul, you know you're supposed to look at other people when they're speaking to you," Brenda intoned predictably. "I don't think you're even listening."

Paul got up and began moving toward the shelves with the math kits and equipment.

"Paul, *sit* down. The teacher didn't say you could get up yet."

So it continued until I could take the incessant buffeting no longer. Thankfully, it was a spectacular fall day. I suggested we take a walk around the neighborhood, guessing correctly that Brenda would want to remain behind to keep an eye on little Tina.

As we meandered up Wilbur Street, I found myself wondering what it must be like to be inside Paul's skin when his mother goes at him that way. Sitting there at that table with the two of them, I had experienced viscerally the impact of her constant managing. It certainly made me feel jumpy—and I'd had to endure only ten minutes of it. Could six years' worth be part of the cause of Paul's so-called hyperactivity?

Wanting to better understand the interaction I had witnessed between Paul and his mom spurred me to spend several Saturday afternoons poring through the medical journals in the Albany Medical Center Library, where I happened on two landmark investigations into the possible psychological origins of ADHD by psychologists Elizabeth Carlson, Deborah Jacobvitz, and Alan Sroufe. Two things set their work apart from the bulk of the research to date. Whereas almost all previous studies focused on children who had already been diagnosed and then searched backwards for causes, Carlson, Jacobvitz, and Sroufe's was an examination of nearly three hundred mothers and their infants selected from public health clinics in Minneapolis. The authors followed the children forward to age six to see who developed ADHD behaviors and then tried to ascertain why.

Another unique aspect of Carlson, Jacobvitz, and Sroufe's work is that it marked the first time anyone included the direct observation of the *quality* of mother-infant interactions. All previous studies of possible nonbiological contributions to ADHD limited themselves to quantitative factors such as socioeconomic status, parental psychiatric history, and parent questionnaires and interviews obtained after the fact of a child's assessment and labeling.

In their first study, published in 1987 in the journal *Child Development*, the three psychologists attempted to determine the role of early childhood "arousal regulation" in the development of hyperactivity, which is considered a central component of the ADHD syndrome.[2] In phase one, for instance, researchers observed both feeding and play situations in the homes of the subjects at age six months, recording the extent to which the mother disrupted the baby's ongoing activity rather than adapt the timing and quality of her initiations and interventions to the infant's mood and current interests. Here they found that maternal disruption of an infant's efforts to modulate and control his or her own level of arousal—by doing things such as shoving a bottle into the child's mouth despite the child's efforts to push it away, or stimulating rather than soothing an already overaroused infant, and other forms of overly controlling or chaotic care—unwittingly inhibits the development of a child's ability to regulate his or her own impulses, to tolerate frustration, and to sustain focus. The effect is particularly acute, they determined, during the stages in infancy and early childhood when the child is ready to take the next developmental step toward greater independence and maturity.

The three psychologists also reported that distractibility, considered a precursor of hyperactivity, was "significantly predicted" by maternal anxiety or aggression, and that "maternal variables significantly predicted distractibility *for boys*" (emphasis mine).

Paul clearly benefited from the freedom of movement and the absence of constant supervision at our school. He appeared more and more at ease, and by the end of his week's trial visit, he had begun making friends with Luis, a nervous, aloof Hispanic boy who also had an anxious, overbearing single mother. The two boys suited each other perfectly, and, as children so often do, they must have shared some invisible sense of a common predicament.

Meanwhile, it was clear to me that we were going to have to find a way to help Paul's mother relax her controlling style of parenting and allow him to become his own manager. How we would do that would remain to be seen, but the situation was so extreme that there could be no avoiding it.

Unfortunately, we wouldn't get the opportunity to work with Brenda on her parenting, because their plans to move to the city fell through and we never heard from them again. I've always regretted that Paul wasn't able to remain with us, because he was a fascinating child and would have thrived, I think, in our energetic, flexible, individually geared environment. But I remain thankful for the vivid examples that both Paul and his mother provided us, ones that clarified and sharpened our thinking about similar families with whom we have dealt, and with whom —increasingly, it appears—we will be dealing in the future.

Anthony was another of our Ritalin boys who, even though he stayed with us for only a year, helped me understand more about the psychological dimensions of ADHD. A nine-year-old African-American boy who attended our school several years before Paul, Anthony resembled Paul in many ways. Like Paul, Anthony was a highly agitated, speedy, anxious child whose wherewithal to attend to his experience was so truncated that he couldn't even stay with the things he enjoyed for longer than five or ten minutes at a time. I remember once, early on, when I was helping Anthony to build something in the woodshop, he would stop what he was doing every few minutes in order to ask me if he could go to the corner store to buy some candy with the dollar his father had given him.

It was Anthony's father who had enrolled Anthony in the Free School. Earl had just assumed custody of his son after Anthony's mother, who had been struggling with drug addiction since before Anthony was born, reentered a drug rehabilitation program in another city. The stormy marriage between Anthony's parents had ended before his third birthday, when Earl left and Anthony remained living with his mother.

Earl, a handsome, impeccably dressed man in his late thirties, was approaching the task of full-time parenting with a great deal of energy and conviction. He was determined to help Anthony reverse his history of school misbehavior and failure. Like Damian's mother, Earl reacted with elation when I informed him that Anthony would have to stop taking Ritalin immediately in order to come to the Free School. A recovering addict himself who then became a drug addiction counselor, he told me in no uncertain terms that he was unwilling to continue administering to Anthony—labeled with ADHD in first grade—a drug so similar to the ones that he was trying to prevent his clients from using.

During Anthony's first days with us, we left him free to zoom around the school at his own frenetic pace. Blessed with real acrobatic skill, he would often spend long periods launching himself off the mini-tramp into a series of amazing flips and somersaults. Thankfully, Earl appeared unconcerned that his son was choosing to take a vacation from traditional schoolwork. Instead he told us how relieved he was that the steady stream of complaints from teachers and administrators had finally stopped.

Anthony's pace began to slow dramatically as he fell into a close friendship with another boy his age. Raman loved art and was quite talented. Before long, Anthony could be seen sitting head to head with him for an hour or more at a time while the two boys worked together on a series of elaborate action scenes. Anthony's much lower skill level seemed to pose no problems. Under Raman's tutelage, he improved quickly. Anthony, meanwhile, continued to keep up his gymnastics routine, and, in turn, began to teach Raman, who was much less physically adept, how to turn front flips.

The two boys became inseparable, as well as, at times, insufferable. Raman, though never labeled, had had trouble fitting in at his previous schools too, and neither boy exactly became an angel overnight with us. Their treatment of the girls in the class was less than noteworthy. What did impress me, however, was the way Anthony's attention span for other things began to stretch out as the duration of his drawing sessions with Raman lengthened. Anthony was growing visibly calmer and more likable by the day.

I will never cease to be amazed at how far Anthony came during the brief year he spent with us. By June he could be found sitting in one place and doing activities other than drawing or gymnastics for as long as forty-five minutes. His impulsive flightiness had become a relic of the past.

During the summer, Anthony, reunited with his neighborhood pals, decided he wanted to return to his old school in order to be with them during the school day. He would come back to visit the Free School—and especially Raman—many times over the next couple of years and proudly let it be known that he was now succeeding in a regular classroom—without Ritalin.

Another study conducted by the aforementioned Paul Jensen applies very directly to Anthony's situation. In an attempt to explore the possible correlation between ADHD and "events that may increase the child's anxiety or threaten the stability of the relationship between parent and child," Jensen compared the developmental histories of thirty-eight children, thirty-two boys and six girls, all diagnosed with ADHD, against the same number of boys and girls who were considered "normal."

The striking results of Jensen's study were published in the *Journal of the American Academy of Child and Adolescent Psychiatry.*[3] Jensen found that the children in the ADHD group suffered a significantly higher number of "threats to attachment," as he termed them. For example, 23.7 percent of the ADHD kids experienced significant separation from caregivers during their childhood, compared to 2.6 percent of the control group. Divorced parents were the norm for 21.1 percent of the ADHD kids, compared to 0 percent of the control group. In the homes of 36.8 percent of the ADHD kids were parents who fought, versus the situation for 2.6 percent of the normal kids, while 55.3 percent of the ADHD group came from families with suspected abuse or neglect, as compared with 15.8 percent of the non-ADHD group.

My experience with Anthony, and with countless others with histories of the emotional, and sometimes physical neglect and abuse that stem from drug addiction, marital discord, and economic stress, confirms the results of the Jensen study. Certainly in Anthony's case, the extreme restlessness and impulsivity he exhibited when he arrived at our doors told the story all too well.

Meanwhile, Jensen's study was influenced by the work of the British psychiatrist John Bowlby, who theorized that the "patterns of attachment" between children and their parents or parent figures play a significant role in determining children's psychological development. Bowlby concluded that there are three principal patterns of attachment present during childhood, and that the patterns are profoundly influenced by the way a child's parents treat him.[4]

Only one of the patterns is consistent with healthy development, while the other two are predictive of disturbed development. It is children with a pattern of "secure attachment"—that is, kids who are confident that their parents will be available, responsive, and helpful when they encounter adverse or frightening situations, who will feel "bold in their explorations of the world and also competent in dealing with it." According to Bowlby, it is primarily the mother who promotes this pattern in the early years by being readily available and sensitive to her child's signals when he or she seeks protection, comfort, or assistance.

The second pattern, "anxious resistant attachment," is caused by a parent who is inconsistently available and who uses threats of abandonment as a means of control. This uncertainty leaves a child anxious, clingy, and prone to separation anxiety. The third pattern is called "anxious avoidant attachment" and is the result of the child's expectation that he or she will be rebuffed rather than nurtured when seeking comfort or protection. Repeated rejection can cause a variety of personality disorders, according to Bowlby.

Anthony's case fit both of the latter two categories. His mother, due to her ongoing battle with drug addiction, was frequently unavailable. Likewise, his father was a transient figure in Anthony's life until he recently assumed full-time custody. Furthermore, the parenting style of Anthony's mother and father when they were available earlier in Anthony's childhood was very likely to have been an authoritarian one, with a scarcity of nurturing and with discipline often coming in the form of threats of abandonment. Bowlby noted that in families in which care-giving arrangements remain stable, a pattern of secure attachment, once formed, tends to be a lasting one. He calls this the establishment of a "secure base." Children who have one will be far more resilient intellectually, emotionally, and immunologically.

Bowlby went on to say that mothers who discourage their children's desire for autonomy and exploration generally are individuals who lacked a secure base during their own childhoods. As a result, they tend, consciously or unconsciously, to invert the parent/child relationship by making their children their own attachment figures, and are therefore far more likely to spoil them. This, then, contributes to the development of a vicious cycle whereby whiny, anxious kids or angry, aggressive ones elicit negative responses from their mothers, thus contributing to the persistence of poor attachment.

Negative patterns of attachment are not irreversible, concluded Bowlby. If the parents start to treat the child differently on a consistent basis, the pattern will change accordingly. However, as children grow older, both the patterns of attachment and the accompanying personality traits become "increasingly a property of the children themselves," and more and more resistant to change. One reason for this is that negatively attached children tend to impose those same patterns on subsequent relationships with authority figures such as teachers, leading to the creation of additional negative feedback loops in school.

Anthony is an excellent example of the reversibility of negative attachment patterns. Once Anthony's father provided his son with the secure base he had never before enjoyed, Anthony was able to relax and shed many of his old dysfunctional behaviors.

Anthony's dramatic turnaround also highlights the tremendous value of a father—or father figure—in the balanced development of a child, especially a boy. One commentator on the subject of behavioral labeling has humorously suggested that ADD be renamed DADD—Dad attention deficit disorder. I couldn't agree more. In every single case at the Free School in which children exhibit behaviors that would get them labeled elsewhere, there has been either a broken or weakened connection with the father. Sometimes the break is obvious: The dad has gone out of the child's life entirely or he is a negative or even harmful presence. In other instances it is subtler. The dad is too busy or self-involved to give his kids the attention they need, or perhaps he is inadvertently passing on the legacy of a disturbed or distant relationship with his father.

In Anthony's case, his father had already initiated the changes that would relieve Anthony's distress. What was needed from the Free School was support in the form of confirmation that Anthony was not suffering from some sort of organic or genetic disorder, and a school environment in which Anthony could repair his self-esteem and learn how to invest himself in his own passions.

8

The long winter months are a time to settle in and focus on indoor projects. Brian and his classmates are busy making arrangements for the big spring trip that the seventh and eighth graders take every year. This time they have decided to attend the annual conference of the National Coalition of Alternative Community Schools, which is being held at a conference center high up in the Rocky Mountains above Denver, Colorado. The weeklong conferences are very exciting, especially for the teenagers, because students will be coming from alternative schools around the country.

The emerging plan is to take the train from Albany to Denver; spend a day and a night at a public alternative school there; then a week at the conference; and then stop in Chicago on the return leg of the journey to visit more schools and tour around the city for a few days.

The budget for the trip is approaching five thousand dollars, which the class must raise entirely on their own. We do it this way for two reasons: as a challenge to the kids, and so that no one will be excluded for financial reasons. The class has already held one successful fundraiser—a fish fry dinner followed by a cake auction—and has several more events in the works: a raffle, selling ad space in their literary magazine, and another benefit dinner at which a raffle drawing will be held. Right now they are in the midst of soliciting prizes from local businesses for the raffle. In years when the kids have been aggressive about getting enticing prizes and selling tickets, raffles have brought in as much as two thousand dollars.

Brian's brashness and ease with people is proving to be a major asset. Whereas kids sometimes tend to be self-conscious and inarticulate at this vulnerable early-teen stage, Brian has no hesitancy whatsoever calling up merchants cold and asking them to donate prizes for the raffle. And he's very good at it. He introduces himself in his most winsome voice, and then his pitch rolls effortlessly off his tongue: "Hi, my name is Brian Anderson and I am an eighth grader at the Free School. This year my class is going to a national alternative education conference in Colorado. We're traveling on Amtrak and the total cost of the trip will be almost five thousand dollars. My classmates and I have to raise all the money by ourselves. One of our fundraisers is a big raffle, and I was wondering if you could please donate something for it."

Some of the kids, especially the first-timers, write their pitches down and then read them shyly to potential donors. But not Brian. He always does his off the cuff, sometimes ad-libbing when he has a particular feel for the person with whom he's speaking. The list of prizes he's already brought in is impressive: a weekend stay in a deluxe hotel, a pearl necklace, and numerous gift certificates to fine restaurants in the area. It's looking good for a lucrative raffle.

Walter, meanwhile, has begun apprenticing at a local computer graphics firm. Ordinarily it is the seventh and eighth graders that become involved in internships and apprenticeships outside of school, but Walter has already moved beyond anything we teachers can do to further his computer skills. Fortunately, the woman who is helping the school to develop its web site has agreed to let Walter work with her in her office every Thursday afternoon for the rest of the school year. It's a great exchange. Walter is drinking up the opportunity to work with a real professional, and Jodie is blown away by this precocious eleven-year-old's knowledge and maturity. In fact, on Walter's first day with Jodie two weeks ago, Jodie was wrestling with a new web page design program she had just installed onto her computer. Walter, already familiar with the software, gave her a quick lesson, saving her considerable time that she would have spent learning the software on her own.

Mark continues to work diligently with Nancy on his reading. His progress is slow but steady, and his determination is unflagging. At this point it's simply a matter of time before he completely cracks the code and is reading confidently on his own.

Just yesterday Mark chaired his third consecutive council meeting, which tend to occur with more frequency as winter drags on and we are all cooped up together. The increasing number of Ritalin kids coming our way and all the restless energy they bring with them doesn't help matters any. I think the kids are electing Mark repeatedly because he's becoming so adept at keeping the proceedings on track. He is able to maintain order without becoming heavy-handed, and frequently he has good suggestions for solving the problem at hand. It's no wonder, given how often he was left to fend for himself and how adroitly he reversed his exile from the Free School.

Thankfully, it appears that Mark's status with us is now secure. His father has remained entirely out of the parenting picture since Mark went to live with his mother, and his mother is thoroughly pleased that Mark is back with us again—especially now that he is making a serious effort to learn how to read.

This morning Damian comes in while I'm typing at our classroom Macintosh. We're in the midst of a thaw, and the kids in my group and in Dave's are up at the park playing a big game of football. Even though the ground is still semifrozen and the temperature is hovering in the thirties, they couldn't wait to get outside on such a crisp, sunny day. I am thoroughly enjoying the quiet and the chance to catch up on some school correspondence.

Damian has been with us for four months now. While he has definitely begun to find his place, thus far he has pretty much stayed away from engaging in physical games and sports. One of the reasons for this, I think, is that he's less coordinated than many of the other kids, meaning that sports don't afford him the same level of superiority and control as a mental game such as D&D. The few times I have seen him try playing a sport, he has tended to drop out as soon as things don't go his way.

With the other kids gone, Damian looks a little lost and like he's searching for something to do. He quickly strikes up a conversation with me about dogs. His dog recently had puppies, and he wants to tell me about their comical antics. Our fast-paced chat is punctuated with his requests to take down one or another of the science kits that line the shelves above the computer desk. I notice something I've observed about Damian on previous occasions: Sometimes when he asks a question, he doesn't pause long enough for me to respond.

This time I decide to point out the pattern to him: "You know, Damian, you often don't wait for me to answer you after you've asked me a question."

"Sorry," he replies, a bit chagrined.

"Hey, it's okay; you don't have to apologize," I return. "You're not doing anything wrong. It's just kind of frustrating because it feels as though you're talking *at* me and not *with* me." And then, "Do you understand the difference?"

"Kind of," he answers, looking a little puzzled now.

Making sure to remove any traces of annoyance from my

voice, I ask, "Do you know what that's about for you?"

"I don't know," he says, thinking out loud. "I just really wanted to tell you about the puppy that got trapped behind my bed last night. He whined and whined, and we didn't know if we would ever be able to get him out."

"It sounds like you're so excited about what you're going to tell me next that you don't want to have to stop long enough for me to answer you," I suggest.

Damian shrugs. "I guess."

"Do you think you could start trying to notice when you've asked me something and then give me a chance to talk?" I inquire. "It's not a big deal, but I'd appreciate it if you would."

"Sure," he returns, seeming at ease now with our exchange.

I decide to shift the conversation to the soon-to-arrive new human member of his family. "How are you feeling about your mother having a baby?"

"I can't wait," he bursts out. "Babies are so cool."

Damian's behavior has been deteriorating for the past couple of weeks. He's been on edge a good deal and has been showing increasing disrespect toward the preschool teachers—all women this year—when he's gotten too rowdy and they've had to tell him to go back downstairs. We suspect the reason for his regression has to do with mounting anxiety over the coming sibling.

I want to make sure he isn't lumping babies into the same mental category as puppies. So I come back with, "Yeah, babies are a lot of fun. But they can also be a real pain in the neck—especially when they cry in the middle of night and wake everyone up." And then, "Things are really going to change at home after the birth, aren't they?"

"Yeah," he replies. "My mom says she's going to need a lot of help with the baby."

I tell him what a fine big brother he'll make and then ask whether he's wishing for a boy or a girl.

He answers almost instantly, "I want a little sister, definitely."

What a good choice, I think to myself. A girl will represent much less of a threat to his position in the family.

Our conversation drifts off to more mundane matters, and ultimately Damian remembers to follow through on his earlier requests for one of the science boxes. I bring down one on magnetism for him. He spends the next fifteen minutes or so experimenting with the different magnets before he says good-bye and heads back to his own classroom.

I'm glad for the opening to talk to Damian about the new baby on the way. Major changes very often throw vulnerable children even further off balance, and Damian, after ten years of enjoying his mother's exclusive attention, is almost certain to experience the sudden arrival of a cute, diaper-clad rival as a major change. My hope is that, as this new chapter in his life unfolds, he will be able to talk about the upsetting parts as well as the delightful ones.

It's not hard to imagine why someone might conclude that Damian has a short attention span, an "attention deficit." He tends to move rapidly from one activity to the next, and he has a habit of asking questions that never get answered. Also, in a room full of people, he is highly reactive to novel stimuli. His attention can shift almost automatically from what he was previously focusing on to any new sound or movement.

But does Damian *have* something called an "attention deficit," or *is* he simply an impatient, impulsive, or hyperalert person? I don't think I'm just splitting hairs here. Declaring that

Damian *has* an attention deficit amounts to the leap of converting an adjective—impatient, impulsive, hyperalert—into a noun: short attention span. It is prescriptive rather than descriptive, meaning that it inflates a personal characteristic—impulsive—into a medical condition: "attention deficit."

The problem, according to Ivan Illich, lies in the modern tendency to refer to the body as though it were a machine.[1] Even the health terminology we use today comes from physics, not biology. Fear, worry, anxiety, uncertainty are now all generically referred to as "stress," which is an engineering concept. Instead of looking at the body's many individual ways of defending itself against pathogens, we speak of an "immune system." Or consider the cover headline of a recent *Newsweek* magazine announcing an article on the subject of ADHD: "How to Build a Better Boy."[2]

The semantic difference between *having* something and *being* it is significant, because if you *have* something, such as a headache, then you can take something to relieve it, such as an aspirin. If, on the other hand, you *are* impatient, then you have a choice: Either you can go on being that way or you can decide to make an effort to be more patient in the future.

This kind of change involves two elements, awareness and volition, which is why from time to time I will continue to bring it to Damian's attention when he does things such as rush past his own questions before they can be answered. My purpose isn't to nag him into a more correct way of communicating, but rather to help him to construct an awareness of his mode of being in the world of others. He knows I won't be grading his performance. Rather, the context for this kind of interaction is our relationship, nothing more, and my concern here has to do with the quality of our exchanges. For them to improve, Damian will need to expand his awareness beyond his customary self-centered, impulsive point of reference. Then he will need ample opportunity to experiment with alternative behaviors. Ultimately, either he will choose to be different or he won't.

A third element in successfully making what might be called "character changes" is identifying the causes of a given troublesome pattern—if indeed it is troublesome—and when possible, alleviating them. As I said earlier, two reasons for Damian's hurriedness, distractibility, and single-mindedness are his high level of anxiety and his social inexperience. There is every reason to believe that, given sufficient exposure to the types of influences in school that I have already described, as well as greater stability at home—once he adjusts to no longer being the only child—Damian will grow less anxious and more adept at making satisfying connections with others.

Talks about the new baby notwithstanding, Damian's hostility toward the female teachers continues to escalate. Today he is sent downstairs for the umpteenth time, in this instance by Rene, the youngest preschool teacher. Before exiting he apparently turned and defiantly muttered a number of disrespectful expletives while delivering the basic message: "You're a woman and I don't have to listen to you."

Rene follows Damian down the stairs and immediately calls a council meeting. This time the topic of discussion becomes Damian's attitude toward Rene and the other female teachers, rather than how he interacts with the preschoolers. Because Rene is very popular with all of the kids, Damian, once again, is on precarious footing.

Rene explains to the group that she asked Damian to leave because he had instigated a stuffed animal throwing battle among the four- and five-year-olds. She then provides us with a somewhat censored sampling of the names he called her and says that she and the other teachers upstairs have had it with him. They can no longer trust him around their little charges, and whenever they've had to stop him lately, he has gotten nasty.

Damian is spitting mad and has little to say for himself. One of the older boys, thinking on his feet, asks, "What's up, Damian? I've never heard of you talking that way to Dave, or Lex, or Jeff, or Chris."

Damian tries to ignore the question, but after a little more pushing and prodding from the group, the real truth comes spurting out. Damian thrusts up his hand and is recognized by the chair. "I hate women, except for my mother," he vehemently declares. "I love her."

One of the kids, with all of a seven-year-old's innocent power of perception, immediately asks, "But your mother is a woman—why don't you hate her, too?

Damian is in no mood for psychology, or logic, either. He sits with his arms loudly folded across his chest and refuses to look at anyone. This is about as angry as I have seen him, a sure sign, believe it or not, that we are beginning to get somewhere.

Rene, sensing accurately that there's not likely to be any happy ending to this council meeting, makes a motion that Damian has to stay away from the upstairs kids, and their teachers, until further notice, or until he initiates sitting down with the teachers and thoroughly talking the matter through privately.

One of Damian's classmates, feeling some compassion for Damian's predicament, asks him if he has any ideas of his own about how to resolve the problem. The gesture is met only with silence, and the motion carries unanimously.

The situation only continues to deteriorate. With the warmer temperatures, the preschoolers are starting to spend a lot of time outside on the school's backyard playground. We frequently find Damian sneaking outside to be with them. When confronted, he plays innocent and tries a legalistic defense: "Oh, I thought I wasn't allowed *upstairs*." When that doesn't wash, he returns to his earlier mouthy defiance.

There are closed doors to keep Damian out of the preschool during winter. But when spring arrives, the four downstairs doors to the backyard will generally remain wide open in order to clear out the stale air of the long winter. Short of tying Damian up or locking him in a room, there will be no way to keep him from mixing with the little kids in the yard, other than repeatedly sending him in after he has been discovered. The freedom in the school, as can be seen so clearly in this case, is dependent on a high degree of trust and mutual respect. When an angry, stubborn child like Damian elects to persist in challenging whatever limits we set for him, it thrusts us squarely onto the horns of a dilemma: Do we continue trying to rein him in, or do we send him back to the kind of regulated, highly supervised environment from whence he came?

A week of unseasonable weather brings the problem to a head and leaves Nancy, Dave, and me jointly pondering the question of what to try next. I recall his mother, Paula, informing us at the post-trial conference that Damian was in counseling, so we decide to call an emergency meeting with Paula and the therapist. I strongly encourage Paula to invite her boyfriend, Joe, who has become a stepdad to Damian and is the father of the new baby.

Joe consents to come, and we meet with the therapist, whom Paula and Damian call Dr. D, at school the following afternoon. I open the conference by saying the last thing we want to do is give up on Damian. We've made real progress helping him to curb his aggressive behavior, and his overall demeanor has calmed considerably. But his recent refusal to adhere to the policy regarding him and the preschool kids and staff presents us with an impossible situation. Nancy adds that because all three preschool teachers are women, with their hands full even when Damian isn't around, something has got to give.

The first important information to come out is that Damian's counseling visits have been very sporadic and he has had only a handful of sessions since the beginning of the school year. Apparently the therapist moved his office across the river and is now substantially farther away than he used to be. The combination of Paula's advancing pregnancy and an unreliable car has resulted in many missed appointments. Also, the therapist recently changed insurance groups, thus muddying the financial picture and making the counseling difficult for Paula to afford.

Both Dr. D, a gentle-mannered man in his late forties, and Paula make a commitment to seeing to it that Damian has weekly sessions in order to raise his level of emotional support during this crisis period. Joe volunteers that he has a car now and offers to drive Damian to Dr. D's office.

Paula shares that Damian is regressing at home, too. He has begun talking back to her again and refusing to comply with household chores and routines. We all agree that the pregnancy is probably causing Damian's anxiety to spike back up to old levels. Thinking out loud, Dr. D says that Damian's hostility toward women hasn't as yet come up in their sessions but that now he will try to steer their work in that direction. Observing that Damian has made positive changes since he began attending the Free School, he encourages us to find a way to bear with Damian through this narrow passage.

We learn from Dr. D that he was Damian's therapist last year when Damian was "on medication," but that he fully supported

Paula's attempt to take him off. He says he thinks the Free School's autonomy-based approach is exactly right for Damian at this point, and that he just needs more time in this kind of environment.

Wanting to address the situation with Damian at home—and take full advantage of Dr. D and Joe's presence—I ask Dr. D about the idea of Joe being the one who gets Damian to do his chores and to whom Damian comes when he needs to ask permission for something. Dr. D agrees with me that it would be an excellent way to shift Damian's negative focus away from his mother and to prepare for the baby's arrival, when Paula will of necessity be less available to her firstborn. Perhaps it will help in some indirect way to reduce Damian's hostility toward the preschool teachers, too.

The conference ends on a hopeful note. We're grateful to Damian's therapist for taking time out of a very busy schedule to meet with us on such short notice. In a private follow-up discussion, Nancy and I decide that it is too soon to throw in the towel. Our optimism, however, remains guarded, given how difficult Damian is becoming.

Without a doubt, biopsychiatric drugs are an expedient route to controlling children who, for whatever reasons, have difficulty controlling themselves. But at what price? A high one, I say. Far too high. Drugging Damian represented a final judgment that he was biologically incapable of managing his own impulses and learning to make responsible choices.

At the Free School, we don't treat the Ritalin kids any differently from the rest. We find that all children are capable of a high degree of responsibility and self-regulation. Happy, untraumatized children who have been raised to be self-regulating tend to be naturally responsible and independent. Kids who have not been raised this way need a patient, forgiving setting in which to learn. Those who have suffered significant distress in addition to having a history of being overmanaged have a great deal more to learn than the rest.

Kids who are at the mercy of a cacophony of impulses, or whose perceptual apparatus is scrambled and confused, need time to decompress and explore their inner as well as outer worlds. That is why we don't micro-educate the mind. We have learned over the years that hungry, activated minds don't need to be taught everything; they will seek out information and generate new ideas and connections as the situation calls for them.

It is essential, in the case of kids like Damian with a history of labeling and drugging, to allow them to find their own level, to begin by learning to meet their most pressing needs first. Damian came to us all tied up in knots. The "symptoms" for which he was previously medicated were distress signals, and we believe that real growth or healing cannot occur if these signals are masked over with drugs. Just as a wise physician will hold off treating a fever that is a response to an infection in the body and instead allow the infection to run its course so that it can bolster the body's natural immunity, we know that we must allow Damian's anger and hostility to surface and, in a sense, run its course. In this instance, the cost that must be carefully monitored is whether or not Damian is infringing too heavily on the other kids. He is walking precariously close to that fine line at present. Hopefully all of our concerted efforts can keep him from stepping over it.

Meanwhile, there has been considerable improvement in William's behavior since the beginning of the year. He seems much happier and more relaxed, and he is definitely getting a feel for directing himself and managing his impulses. His lessons in limits continue, however. Today I discover that he has skipped out on a council meeting, successfully hiding in his classroom while the meeting took place without him. Attendance at council meetings is required. I warn William that at the next meeting from which he is absent without excuse I'm likely to make a motion that he won't be able to swim when we go to the pool again but will have to sit on the bench and watch instead. His apparent lack of concern is not a good sign. One can only wonder how much longer he will go on testing every limit in sight.

He certainly isn't done with his classmates. We were hopeful when two new boys joined his class during the preceding weeks that William might begin making some friends. He and Pierre have made cautious progress toward that end—with Pierre providing much of the impetus—but Pierre's parents have announced that they will be moving back to Canada soon. Unfortunately, the two new boys have struck up an instant friendship with each other, and William doesn't seem to know how to get in with them. He has begun bugging the girls instead.

William quickly learns it is a mistake to pick on Carl's sister, Lamika, who, while afraid of many things, is not the least bit intimidated by bigger boys. She puts up with a day or two of William's testing, but when he persists this morning, her cry of "COUNCIL MEETING!" rings out around the school.

Once again there's no sign of William. This time I suspect his motivation has little to do with trying to get away with not attending another meeting. He's not here, I am quite sure, because he knows what's in store for him. Lamika tells the only side of the story there is to be told, and several of us question her to make certain she wasn't provoking William. All of the other kids in the class report that Lamika had done nothing to him other than repeatedly tell him to stop bothering her. The general consensus of the meeting is that this is an appropriate occasion to invoke Pierre's earlier motion regarding William's bullying of smaller kids, that it seems to be the only way he will ever learn. While Lamika is choosing her helpers—the same five kids who helped Pierre to sit on William—I privately decide against carrying out my threat to make a motion against William for skipping council meetings. He's in enough trouble already.

Immediately following the meeting, Lamika and her deputies dash off to look for William. But he's nowhere to be found. Although I happen to know he has secreted himself behind the open door to his classroom, when the group of searchers asks me if I have seen him, I lie and shake my head. I figure it's best to milk this drama for all it is worth, because William has already been sat on twice and we never want to see such a drastic consequence become routine. If he doesn't get the message this time, then we will have to come up with another way to persuade him to stop bullying.

The search for William extends throughout the school, with speculation growing that he has run away. Finally, one of the kids thinks to check behind the door, and there is William, looking sheepish. Appearing to accept the justice that awaits him, he makes no attempt to escape; in fact, he practically helps the group to sit on him.

As soon as they have William secured on the rug, he blurts out tearfully, "Okay! Okay, I'll stop. I promise I won't bother you anymore, Lamika."

Lamika and the others let William up as gently as they had set him down, and the whole group, William included, resumes working on the collage project they were starting when the trouble began.

When William comes through my classroom later in the morning, he tells me about the incident without any hint of fear or shame.

"This time they only had to sit on me for a minute," he proudly announces.

"Do you think they'll need to sit on you again?"

"No way!"

It is a prediction that will prove to be quite accurate.

When dealing with children as willful as William, very often more is not better. If this had not turned out to be the last time he attempted to bully another child, then we would have abandoned the intervention of having his peers sit on him, done some creative thinking, and tried something else.

Several days later William skips out on another council meeting. Because this one has nothing to do with him, it's time for me to follow through on my earlier threat to make a motion barring him from swimming. Unbeknownst to William, the motion passes unanimously, and I volunteer to deliver the bad news.

As fate would have it, today just so happens to be a swimming day. I decide to wait until after lunch to tell William about the motion so that he won't spend the morning stewing over missing out on one of his favorite activities.

Later, when I inform him about the council meeting decision, his face falls momentarily. But like a true warrior, he recovers quickly, shooting back, "I'm not going to the pool. You can't make me." This becomes his mantra right up until everyone is ready to head off to the pool.

William, true to his word, refuses to accompany the others. Dave has to carry him out to the van and then into the pool building, with William still screaming, "You can't make me go! You can't make me go!"

The lifeguard, a veteran employee of this century-old inner-city institution, isn't fazed in the least by William's histrionics. Soon the angry boy's protests are lost among the echoing shouts of twenty kids plunging merrily into the brisk water. The sight of the rest of the group having so much fun in the pool without him drives William into an even greater rage. Dave, sitting next to William on the bench, gently gathers him up in his arms so that in the safety of his lap William can really let loose. Dave holds William so that William's chest is right up against his own, with William's legs straddled around his hips.

As William's yelling begins to take on a roaring quality, Dave says to him, "William, you sound just like a lion."

William roars on for the next fifteen or twenty minutes, filling the old building with the music of his rage. When the energy of his anger is finally spent, a wave of fear washes over him. He is soundless now, his face contorted, tears streaming down.

Then he starts to struggle again, crying out repeatedly, "Please let me go, Dave. I can't breathe."

Dave checks to make sure he isn't holding William too tightly. He whispers soothingly into William's ear, "You're doing fine, William. You were really mad, and now you're feeling frightened."

"Dave, you gotta let me go; my brain hurts," William continues. "I'm gonna die. I'm gonna die."

"It's all right, William," Dave replies. "You're not going to die, but getting as angry as you did can be pretty scary. I'm just going to hold you a little while longer until you feel okay again."

William's bout with terror passes more quickly than his

rage. His entire body grows relaxed and heavy, and he allows Dave to rock him and softly stroke his head and shoulders until it's time to return to school.

Here again, William is the subject of a drastic physical intervention that we reserve for extreme situations. It's simply called "holding," a therapeutic technique that we borrowed from settings that deal with emotionally disturbed children. The idea is for the intervening adult to gather in a child who is bursting at the seams with pent-up anger and enable him to release the emotional pressure without doing harm to himself or others. I should note that it is imperative that the adult not be feeling angry or disapproving, or be expecting a particular behavioral outcome from the child. Strange as it may seem, this kind of holding is a loving act, and the purpose is solely to help children vent their stored-up anger safely.

But how did William come to be so full of rage at such an early age? Part of the answer, I think, lies in his growing up in a household where he is punished frequently and sometimes severely. Thankfully, William Senior assures us that he no longer "whoops" his sons. The trouble with physical punishment is that it can be a humiliating and frightening experience, leaving the child angry and resentful, and often only serving to reinforce the behavior the parent is trying to stop. William's father is a large, intimidating man. It could be quite dangerous for William to express to his dad his anger at being threatened, spanked, or hit with a belt. Therefore, William has had to learn to swallow his rage, with his tightly muscled chest and throat preventing him from expressing the powerful emotions that are now locked inside him.

But Dave is anything but a strict, imposing presence. William knew instinctively that it was safe to let go while Dave held him in his lap, and let go he did. By the time William was done, his ordinarily taught musculature was soft and loose, leaving William undefended and open to receiving Dave's comforting tenderness.

William faithfully attends the next several council meetings. Unfortunately, he's doing his damnedest to make us wish he weren't at these meetings, and chairpersons are finding it increasingly difficult to keep him in order. I have no trouble understanding that William doesn't want to sit through discussions of other people's problems; but then again, the rest of the six-year-olds all manage to do it. No ground will be conceded to William here because, more than anything else, the council meeting system insures that the school functions as a true community and not just a chaotic collection of individuals.

Today when he disrupts the proceedings yet again, I move to amend my previous motion about William skipping meetings. I propose that if William's behavior in a council meeting is so disruptive that the chair has to remove him, then he should suffer the same consequences as he does when he skips a meeting. The motion passes without discussion, and I notice a sober expression settle in on William's face. His demeanor for the remainder of the meeting is exemplary.

At the following council meeting, however, which doesn't occur for a number of days, William reverts to his old ways. I suggest to the chairperson that she remind William of the new motion, but this only slows him down for a short while. It's not long before she is forced to direct William to a folding chair in the kitchen, placed there just for this purpose.

Much to everyone's surprise, William willingly accompanies the others out to the van for the next swimming expedition, even though he knows he will have to watch from the bench again. This time Dave joins the kids in the pool while I sit out with William, whose shift in strategy is remarkable. Within minutes he calmly leaves the bench and strays over to the edge of the pool, looking at me all the while for a reaction. Since we are at the shallow end and there are no serious safety concerns, I decide to look the other way.

Next William tries everything he can think of to get the attention of the kids in the pool, but he has little success. Even name-calling and rude gestures fall short because the kids are lost in the magic of the warm blue water.

When I glance over at William to check on him, I see that he is lying down next to the pool—still fully clothed—and is swishing one arm around in the water. His long-sleeved pullover shirt is soaked up to the elbow. Again he looks toward me for a reaction, but instead I turn back toward Dave so that we can resume our conversation. The lifeguard, who is sitting on another bench by the deep end, catches my attention with a puzzled look. I signal back silently that I will handle William. The guard has known us for years and realizes we are a bit on the unconventional side.

William stands back up and sidles over to the stairs in the corner of the pool nearest me. He's less than ten feet away now, so I am sure to notice him as he slides down onto the first step wearing his high-top basketball shoes.

He sends me one of his trademark grins, which I return, saying, "How's the water, William?"

Just as one of the kids calls out to me to watch her do a handstand on the bottom of the pool, I can see out of the corner of my eye that William has gone down a second step. He's wet almost to his knees. It's like a staring contest between two masters of the game. Who will blink first? Thankfully, the rest of the group is still too involved in their water play to react to William's outrageousness. While I'm trying to decide whether I should scream at William to get the hell out of the water or run over and baptize his stubborn little soul, he climbs back up the stairs and begins shaking the water out of his sopping wet sneakers.

When it's time to leave, William happily drips his way out to the van. Fortunately, he took off his coat when we first arrived, and it seems to be keeping him sufficiently warm. I know it will be an interesting discussion with his mom when she comes for him at three o'clock. By now, she too knows that we do things a bit differently.

Back at school a few days later, Lamika calls yet another council meeting, this time about a problem she is having with a girl in the class. Apparently Kathy has defaced a drawing that Lamika put a great deal of time and effort into creating, and to make matters worse, Kathy is refusing to deal with the issue other than to keep repeating, "I didn't do it and I don't care."

Despite the fact that Kathy's stonewalling causes the council meeting to drag on longer than usual, William does nothing to disrupt it. He even contributes to the discussion, encouraging Kathy to come clean and tell Lamika that she's sorry and won't do it again.

Anyone sitting close enough to him in the circle can hear him saying to himself in a low voice, "I'm not missing swimming ever again."

Now it is William who is being tested, thanks to a sudden rash of council meetings. It is becoming increasingly evident that when the council meetings are relevant to William's concerns, he generally stays right with the proceedings, doesn't distract from them, and even participates on occasion. When the issues raised in the meetings don't have much to do with him, however, he quickly grows bored and restless. William isn't the only younger student for whom this is the case, and we try to allow them a fair amount of leeway. It remains to be seen whether the prospect of losing his swimming privileges will provide sufficient motivation to get him through the meetings in which he has little interest.

Perhaps in recognition of his improved council meeting behavior, today William is nominated for chairperson for the first time. Though he isn't elected, he is clearly quite pleased with himself.

A couple of days later, William himself calls a council meeting. He has just been kicked out of the movie the kids are filming, and he is feeling furious, hurt, and left out all at once. The movie is a cops and robbers action adventure for which some of the older students have written the script. Props have been fashioned out of refrigerator boxes. Everyone in William's class has been given bit parts as members of a roaming gang of thieves, but William apparently isn't satisfied with his limited role. After he is warned numerous times to stop disrupting the rehearsals, this morning his loud wisecracks and blasts of imaginary gunfire got him thrown off the set for good by the two ten-year-old girls who initiated the project.

William states his problem clearly, and in return the girls passionately explain to him why they booted him out.

"We're sorry you can't be in the movie, but we're tired of you interrupting all the time."

Wisely, William refrains from arguing and instead puts on a wounded, rejected look.

As the meeting is drawing to a close, he raises his hand again and asks the girls with just the right amount of deference, "Can

I please have one more chance? Please!"

"One more chance and that's it," comes the firm reply. "And you have to promise not to call another council meeting if we have to kick you out again."

"Okay, I promise," William returns, beaming.

I think everyone is pleased to see William rewarded for calling a council meeting on his own behalf. Perhaps this will strengthen his resolve to behave himself in the meetings that don't concern him.

William gets through the remaining rehearsals without incident. He plays out his role, which involves being arrested and convicted, going to jail, and then busting out in the end, with great energy and flair. The directors have no regrets at having let him back in.

William's round of successes continues. Swimming day arrives, and at the conclusion of one last council meeting before lunchtime, he bursts out with great pride, "I did it! I get to go swimming this week!"

The chair, recognizing the importance of the moment, ignores that William is out of order.

9

The conference with Damian's therapist seems to have taken a little pressure off all concerned. Damian's defiance subsides at least to a manageable level, and Dave is able to pull Damian within the circle of his class with plans for a three-day stay at a wilderness adventure center run by the YMCA. The class will need to raise several hundred dollars to cover the costs of the trip, with each student expected to pull his or her share of the load. This necessitates Damian's participation in numerous class discussions to decide how they are going to come up with the money. Two ideas are finally agreed upon: selling chocolate lollipops donated by a local chocolate factory and publishing a magazine, for which Damian volunteers to write an article.

The wilderness center, located on Lake George in the Adirondack Mountains of upstate New York, features the best high ropes course in the Northeast. One of the girls in the class has announced that she also wants to climb a mountain while they are there. The combination of the challenging activities planned, the prospect of being away from home for three nights, and the pressure on the kids to raise enough money have caused the anxiety level of everyone in the group to rise several notches. One immediate side benefit of the resulting storminess is that it keeps Damian's attention away from the little kids, for the most part, and on his own peer group instead.

Not atypically, it is the boys in the class who seem to have more fear about the trip. And thankfully for Damian, he doesn't appear to be the most frightened. Carl and a new boy in the class are running neck and neck in that contest. Both Carl and Larry have come up with numerous excuses for why they won't be able to go, though both continue to help with the fundraising, which is actually proceeding quite well. Dave is in a dialogue with their parents to ensure that neither boy backs out.

My suspicion is that Carl's real reason for not wanting to go is that he still wets the bed at night—a matter he's not about to discuss openly. I find a quiet moment when Carl is alone and tell him that I wet the bed when I was his age and that it kept me from wanting to go places overnight. I explain that other Free School kids over the years have had the same trouble, and that if he should happen to have a problem while he's at the camp, then Dave will discreetly help him with his night clothing and bedding so that none of the other kids finds out. Carl seems a little more relaxed about the trip by the end of our chat.

Larry, on the other hand, seems to be afraid to be away from his mother for three nights. Larry's mother is overbearing, as well as mentally unstable, and Dave and I surmise that her fragility makes it difficult for Larry to venture out. Here our strategy is largely to skip over Larry and persuade his parents to insist that he participate in the trip. Over the course of several lengthy conversations, Dave finally gets across to them how important it is that their son, who is very unbonded socially, share in this adventure experience with the rest of his class.

Damian, interestingly, is showing no signs of not wanting to participate. Perhaps it's because he is from the Adirondacks and is comfortable being in the woods. In any case, Damian turns out to be one of the more gung-ho members of the group and frequently exclaims how much he is looking forward to the trip.

*   *   *

With March sliding quickly into April, Brian and his classmates are also working to raise money for their Colorado trip. They are making daily sorties downtown to sell books of raffle tickets and magazine ads to stores and businesses. Thus far they have raised enough cash for the train fare, an impressive accomplishment for a group of eight young people, but they have only a little over three weeks left to bring in the cash they will need for food, conference fees, and getting around in Chicago.

The increasing pressure has brought to a head a growing rift within the class. Lately the girls have been doing the bulk of the raffle ticket and ad selling, while the boys always seem to be finding excuses why they can't go out. In Brian's case I don't think the problem is laziness or being spoiled. He worked very hard soliciting the raffle prizes. He's eagerly looking forward to the trip, and I doubt homesickness will be an issue for him. No, my suspicion is that Tyrone is very anxious about traveling all the way to Colorado and being away from home for two weeks —he has begun dropping subtle hints that he may not go—and that is pulling his friend Brian away from the fundraising effort.

It's not uncommon for inner-city children to have fears about extended travel. The safe boundaries of their world tend to be narrowly defined. In Tyrone's case, the move to Albany last year from New York City represents the only time he has ever gone anywhere. And, unfortunately, there is no way this street-tough fourteen-year-old is going to admit his fears to the group. I have even tried talking with him privately, but to no avail.

To avert disaster, last week I advised their teacher Lex to figure out with the kids how much money they still need to raise and then divide the amount by eight. Everyone who raised his or her share would get to go, and the others would have to remain behind. This hopefully will spur the slackers to get back to work, and it will give Tyrone a way out if he decides he needs one. It also means the girls will no longer have to carry the boys.

The dinner the kids are planning as their culminating fundraiser is providing Brian with an opportunity to redeem himself. His mother's boyfriend is a chef at a local four-star restaurant, and Brian has asked Jim to cook with them. Together, Jim and Brian have worked out an ambitious French menu. Brian has dusted off his begging bowl and has been having good luck getting food donated for the dinner, which will have to net at least a thousand dollars in order for the class to reach its goal.

Dave's class, on the other hand, has successfully completed its fundraising for the trip to Camp Chingachgook. Although there were doubts right up to the end, everyone in the class shows up at school on departure day, loaded down with camping gear. The whole building buzzes with the energy of twelve very excited kids.

With the forecast calling for perfect spring weather over the next several days, Dave and my wife, Betsy, who taught in the school for many years and who has volunteered to help chaperone the trip, shoehorn the group and their luggage into the school van and head north toward the mountains. The interpersonal drama begins almost immediately. Damian chooses to sit next to Marie, whom he apparently has been referring to as his girlfriend for some time. This invites the kind of teasing that kids this age almost inevitably get into when boys and girls start pairing up. And it virtually ensures that Damian will act as the lightning rod for the entire group's anxiety.

The worst teasing comes from a forlorn Larry, who, it turns out, also likes Marie. Carl, clearly unsettled about his decision to go on the trip, quickly joins forces with Larry. Damian, with a lifetime of experience of being the odd kid out, plays his part in predictable fashion, calling the other boys all sorts of nasty names.

Dave and Betsy definitely have their hands full as the van giggles, argues, and curses its way up the interstate.

At the camp the group settles into separate boys' and girls' cabins and then meets together on the lawn by the lake for a picnic lunch. The setting is idyllic except for one element: black flies. May is the height of their season here, meaning that swarms of the hungry, biting gnats will be accompanying every outdoor event. An effective insect repellent that Betsy thought to bring along will keep the suffering to a minimum, but before long three of the inner-city girls are refusing to leave the safety of their screened-in cabin, shrieking, "Them bugs! Them bugs!" whenever Dave or Betsy tries to cajole them back outside.

The bickering among the boys escalates into full-blown conflict when Larry discovers that someone has been messing with his things. His mother has apparently sent him with an entire satchel filled with every remedy under the sun, from three kinds of vitamins to calamine lotion to Band-Aids and antibiotic ointment. Now a couple of items are missing. Fortunately, Larry decides to call a council meeting before a fight breaks out between him and Damian, his prime suspect.

Larry informs the assembled group that he has carefully gone through his belongings and cannot find his Vitamin E oil or his sunglasses, and that when he came in to get something, he caught Damian standing next to his bed where the satchel was sitting, unzipped.

"I know it was zipped up when I went out to play," he says.

"Why did your mother send you with all that stuff anyway?" asks Vanessa, who has temporarily forgotten her aversion to the black flies and is irritated instead to be sitting in a council meeting on such a beautiful spring day.

"I don't know," answers Larry. "She's always worrying about me."

Betsy interjects, "The point is that some of Larry's things appear to be missing, and if someone's taken them, then they need to give them back."

"I didn't do it," blurts out Damian, without being directly accused.

"So what were you doing in the cabin next to Larry's bed?" asks one of the other kids.

"How do you know it wasn't Carl? He's always taking people's stuff."

Carl returns, "Don't even try it, Damian. I've been outside playing all afternoon."

And then, "You know you did it because you were pissed as hell at Larry for teasing you in the van."

"I would've been mad, too, if anybody'd been talking about me and my boyfriend that way," chimes in Vanessa, who loves a good argument.

"Everybody hates me!" moans Damian.

"Come on, Damian." says Dave. "First of all, you know that isn't true. Second of all, that's what you always say when you're feeling defensive because you know you've done something wrong."

"And besides," Betsy adds, "this is not what we're here for. I had to pull a lot of strings to get you all in here this week, so that you could have some real grown-up challenges. Not this kind of nonsense."

Before Damian can retreat into his shell, Dave initiates a discussion about the teasing in the van on the way to the camp.

"I know some of you were very reluctant to come on this trip," he says. "And sometimes it seems a lot easier to pick on someone else rather than deal with our own fears. But the whole point of going on the high ropes tomorrow will be to do just that—face your fear and not let it stop you."

"Do we have to do it?" inquires Carl.

"You don't have to do anything you don't want to do while we're here," answers Dave, "except keep yourselves safe and obey all the rules of the camp."

"What are some of the things you're afraid of?" Betsy asks the class.

Vanessa chimes in without hesitation, "I'm afraid of them damn bugs! They act like they're gonna eat me alive."

The group grows quiet, thoughtful. Betsy breaks the silence with another question. "How many of you are afraid of the dark?"

A number of hands shoot up.

"Well, it is going to be very dark at night, this far away from the lights of the city." Betsy continues. "But wait until you see the stars tonight! The sky will be full of diamonds."

Carl raises his hand and volunteers, "I'm scared something bad might happen to my little sister while I'm gone."

"You really look out for Lamika, don't you?" responds Dave. "She's lucky to have a big brother like you."

"I'm really afraid of heights," says Damian. "But I still want to try going up on the ropes tomorrow."

"Well, there won't be any high ropes if Larry doesn't get his belongings back," Dave warns. "Damian, you could save us all a lot of time if you would just admit you took his things and return them."

Damian's hand is at half-mast. "Yeah, I took his stuff," he mutters, and then, his voice rising, "But he asked for it."

"You did say some pretty rotten things, Larry," adds Dave.

This time it's Larry's hand that slowly creeps up. "Sorry, Damian."

The council meeting ends with Damian's promise not to bother Larry's belongings again.

The high ropes prove to be the perfect medicine for this fractious group of children, some of whom are comfortable being in their own skin and others who are quite vulnerable inside theirs. It is a very structured experience that involves performing various high-wire balancing acts while wearing a rock-climbing harness connected by a belay rope to a staff person on the ground. Such inordinate attention is paid to safety that the exercise contains virtually no danger. It certainly doesn't feel that way, however, when you're attempting to traverse a skinny horizontal log suspended thirty feet above mother earth.

The camp staff gives a lengthy demonstration of safety equipment and procedures. After that they lead Dave, Betsy, and the kids through a number of team-building games and problem-solving initiatives that require cooperation and group thinking. At one point the entire group has to fit itself simultaneously onto a two-foot-square wooden platform resting on the ground, a seemingly impossible feat that takes them fifteen minutes of hilarious trial and error before they finally figure out a way to do it.

This is just the warmup for the next challenge, which, at first glance, seems even more improbable than the first. Now Dave, Betsy, and the kids have to find a way to get every member of the group over a sheer, ten-foot-high wooden wall. On the initial go, the kids hastily decide that Betsy and Dave should climb up first so that they can then hoist up the others. The plan proceeds smoothly, until they come to Walter. He is just too heavy for the adults to lift, and the kids remaining on the ground are unable to give him enough of a boost. On the second attempt, the group tries a different strategy. They lift Betsy up first, leaving Dave and the others on the ground to help hoist Walter up to Betsy's down-stretched arms. After much grunting, groaning, and struggle, Walter is standing next to Betsy on the platform. Next to ascend is Dave, and the three big people are easily able to help up the rest. Before long all fourteen are standing together at the top, cheering and applauding their success.

An important reason for the introductory team building is that, when it comes time for the high ropes, it is the job of everyone on the ground to lend emotional support to the people up in the air wrestling with their fears. Each individual challenge is viewed as a group challenge as well. Dave's class unites quickly, a testament, perhaps, to the high degree of cooperation required to raise money for the trip.

The Chingachgook staff invites a third of the group to begin donning harnesses and safety helmets in preparation for climbing up into the trees. Some of the "elements," as the different segments of this aerial obstacle course are called, are more frightening and difficult than others. It is everyone's responsibility to set his or her own goals. Participants are encouraged simply to meet their fear and then try to push themselves a little bit past the point where they feel they can go no further. There is no stigma attached to bailing out if the fear becomes too overwhelming.

Damian elects to go first, wisely selecting a less challenging element, one that involves climbing a giant cargo net twenty-five feet up to a wire cable that stretches another forty feet between two stout pine trees. He ascends about a third of the way before panic sets in. While he clings to the net, shaking all over and refusing to move either up or down, a chorus of encouragement is called up from below.

"You can do it, Damian!"

"Look how far you've gone already!"

"It's okay to be scared, just don't let it stop you."

The Camp Chingachgook group leader reminds Damian that he is connected to a safety line.

"Even if you slip, Damian, I won't let you fall. And you know, since you're almost halfway there, it'll probably be better to finish climbing up rather than try to come back down. It seems scarier, but up is easier."

When Damian takes his next tentative step upward, cheers break out on the ground. Gaining confidence as he goes, he completes the journey without faltering and receives another burst of shouts and applause when he stands up on the high wire, hugging the big pine.

But there's little opportunity to celebrate, because the cargo net was only the preliminary event. Though ropes have been strung on either side of the wire to serve as wobbly handrails, it's a long way across—and a long way down. Damian's rising fear is visible. His eyes widen and his face tightens into a frightened grimace. He is quivering all over.

Again everyone on the ground urges him on.

"See how easily you're able to hold yourself up?" his counselor asks. "That's great. Now turn around and just take one step out so that you can see how the ropes will help you keep your balance. And remember, even if you slip, I've got you covered."

After a long pause, Damian turns slowly, releases the tree, and takes an uncertain step forward. Wire and ropes amplify his trembling, but he manages to remain upright.

The counselor continues her steady stream of supportive affirmations, which are echoed by Damian's classmates on the ground.

"You did it!" she praises. "That first step is always the hardest. Now try to keep your eyes focused on the other tree and head straight for it."

Damian plunges ahead, leaning heavily on the ropes to keep from falling. Somewhere along the way, terror has turned into determination. Before long Damian, grinning widely, has his arms wrapped around the opposite pine. When the sound of the clapping and cheering fades away, he declares that he has had enough and asks to be lowered down.

The day is a succession of similar triumphs for the rest of the group. It ends climactically when Carl, too frightened at first even to climb up onto the course, hops off the tiny, high-altitude tree platform where he has spent the past fifteen minutes staring profoundly off into space and lets gravity suck him down the three hundred meter "zip line." I doubt anyone will ever know just what it was that finally enabled him to take that physical and mental leap of faith.

There are many reasons why we take kids on outdoor adventures, some of which I will delve into shortly, but one near the top of the list is to counteract the insidious effects of television on kids.

Some years ago, my curiosity over whether there might be a connection between prolonged television viewing and some or all of the behaviors and learning deficits associated with ADHD led me to the work of Merrelyn Emery, a social scientist at the Australian National University who was hired by the Australian government in 1973 to study the possible social and educational effects of introducing cable television into Australian society.

The first thing Emery learned is that only scant research had been done on the subject of how television influences children's thinking and behavior. By the time she completed the task of cataloguing and synthesizing the available literature, she would be recognized as one of the leading experts in the field.[1]

Emery's most surprising discovery was that the content of a TV program has far less impact on children than the actual medium, which in and of itself appears to have profound neurological effects on the rapidly developing brains of young children. This is because television's video output, produced by a cathode ray tube flashing at a rate of fifty cycles per second, rapidly desensitizes the centers in the brain responsible for receiving and processing visual information—regardless of what a child is seeing on the screen.

Unfortunately, the apparent power of television to impair cognitive functioning is only half of a very disturbing story. Here Merrelyn Emery is careful to note that some children are more vulnerable to the negative effects of TV than others, depending on a complex mixture of hereditary, familial, and other environmental factors.

Television, in virtually paralyzing the left hemisphere of the brain, appears to have far more than just adverse mental effects on its viewers, especially young ones. There may very well be significant emotional and behavioral effects as well. What seems to happen to children as they watch TV—program content becomes extremely relevant here—is that as the left hemisphere grows increasingly passive, it gives way to the right, the primary task of which is to keep watch for information about the environment to which the left should be alerted. So while the left hemisphere naps, the right continues to tune in to the wash of imagery from the screen, and along with the emotional brain, to react to it internally *as though it were real*. Without any logical, analytical processing by the left hemisphere, the right hemisphere and the emotional brain of a child viewer take the violence that has become such a staple of contemporary children's programming at face value and then attempt to initiate an active motor response, an impossible task without the participation of the idle left hemisphere. The end result: a stimulation-preparation-frustration-action cycle in which television's evocative imagery triggers a host of neurological, muscular, and hormonal reactions in the viewer—all in preparation for an action that almost never takes place, at least not while the TV is still on. In other words, says writer and social critic Martin Pawley, "The real crisis of television begins only after the set is turned off."[2]

Pawley is referring to the fact that the longer children sit in front of their TVs, the longer it takes before they snap out of a state of reduced neocortical control, and the more likely it is that their behavior will be influenced by the material they have been viewing. Thus, it is highly possible that heavy TV viewing is a root cause of "hyperactivity," impulsiveness, and aggressive behavior—again, in certain children.

This is the same conclusion reached by psychologists Dorothy and Jerome Singer. In the late 1970s and early 1980s the Singers conducted a number of extensive research projects to determine the behavioral effects of television viewing on young children. In one longitudinal study, reported in the *Annals of Forensic Psychiatry*, two hundred preschoolers were watched for signs of aggression and heightened motor activity during free-play periods for three two-week intervals over the course of a year.[3] Trained observers, working in pairs, independently recorded all language and behavior. At the same time, the subjects' parents were asked to keep a daily log of their children's TV viewing habits—to record the title of each program and to rate its intensity.

Not surprisingly, a clear-cut linkage was found between the amount of violent programming watched by the children and the degree of aggressive behavior and heightened motor activity in their play. Several of the Singers' earlier studies had already demonstrated the same connection. There was, however, one very unexpected result this time. The Singers discovered, once all the numbers were crunched, that the single best predictor of overt aggression in the pool of test subjects was *how much* Sesame Street *they watched*. Here again was confirmation for Merrelyn Emery that the harmful neurological effects of TV viewing are due more to the medium itself than they are to program content.

Much of the research aimed at documenting the negative effects of television on children is now decades old. In the meantime, the power of TV to arouse children has only continued to grow. This is because, according to Joseph Chilton Pearce, who has spent the past four decades delving into the mysteries of the child mind, the television industry realized all the way back in the 1950s that it was necessary to counter the medium's tendency to put children's brains to sleep—an item of particular concern to advertisers.[4] Making use of its own neurological studies, the industry discovered that by introducing what are known as "startle effects" into children's programming, it could hold a child's attention indefinitely.

A startle effect is anything that triggers the brain into thinking there might be an emergency unfolding and sends it into a state of alertness. Initially, television accomplished this with sudden and dramatic changes in intensity of light or sound and a rapid shifting of camera angles. However, because the brain habituates to these kinds of startles over time and starts to tune out all over again, the television industry has had to up the ante every ten years or so by making the startles bigger and bigger, reaching the point now where there are an average of sixteen bits of violence in every half-hour of children's programming.

Establishing a clear-cut causal relationship between TV and

childhood neurological damage remains an elusive quest. Currently, Dr. Keith Buzzell, author of *The Children of Cyclops: The Human Brain and the Influences of Television Viewing*, is attempting to carry forward the work of Merrelyn Emery and others. His efforts, too, are hampered by scientific resistance and disinterest, and a resulting dearth of hard data. In answer to the question of whether or not prolonged TV viewing causes lasting cognitive or behavioral difficulties in children, Buzzell concludes:

> Understanding the origins of childhood conditions such as ADHD requires wrestling with a morass of clearly interconnected but incredibly complex factors: the increasing fracture of family life, the rising levels of physical, sexual, and emotional abuse, the influences of environmental toxins and estrogen-like substances on brain development, extraordinary sugar intake, and the poorly understood influences of the plethora of electronic devices—TV, computers, and electronic video games. In the end, however, television is the single most pervasive of all of these influences, and the one that has the most direct, immediate effects on the primal neural reactions that can hamper developmental processes in potentially permanent ways.[5]

On the third morning the group awakens early for their final day in the Adirondacks, this time for an unpackaged adventure. Tiffany has successfully infected all of the kids with her itch to climb a mountain. In consultation with the camp staff, Dave learns of a trail not far from the camp that winds its way up 3,600-foot Buck Mountain, which overlooks a beautiful, aquamarine lake. The hike will cover approximately six miles round-trip, and some of it, according to Dave's topographical map, will be quite steep.

With everyone carrying his or her own food and water for the day, the troop sets out after breakfast with great enthusiasm. Tiffany and Larry burst into the lead, setting a pace that no one else can match. Within the first half-mile, their haste causes them to miss a subtle turn in the trail. The rest of the kids, rushing to keep up, follow their self-appointed leaders unquestioningly off into the forest. Betsy and Dave, who have been pulling up the rear to ensure there are no stragglers, confer secretly and decide not to alert the kids to their error, but to wait and see if anyone notices the disappearance of the bright orange trail markers.

It is some minutes before one of the kids finally realizes they are no longer on track and shouts out, alarmed, "Hey, we're not on the trail anymore!"

"Tiffany! Larry! You better get back here, because we're lost," Vanessa yells ahead to the two ambitious leaders.

When the group reassembles and everyone is accounted for, Dave asks calmly, "What should we do now?"

Tiffany is the first to answer. "I think we should walk back the way we came until we see a marker."

"We could do that," responds Dave, "but the trouble is we may have wandered pretty far off the trail and might not be able to retrace our steps all that well. Then we'll be just as lost as we are now."

Dave notes that several kids, especially Damian and Larry, are starting to look a little panicky.

"But listen, you're never really lost when you have a compass and a good map," he adds quickly, retrieving both items from his knapsack.

"Where are we?" one of the kids asks Dave as he unfolds the map.

"I don't know exactly, but the map shows the trail up the mountain heading west," Dave says. "And if you look here at the compass, you can see that we've been moving to the north. So which way should we walk in order to cross the trail?"

"South?" answers Tiffany.

Dave nods. "Right, and if we keep watching the compass and moving in that direction, then sooner or later we will pick up the trail," he explains. "We all need to keep our eyes open for those orange blazes."

The group heads off again, more slowly this time, with Dave in the lead. Tiffany remains tight by Dave's side so that she has a good view of the compass. Larry, so eager before, hangs back in the rear on one side of Betsy, complaining over and over, "My feet hurt and I want to go back now." Damian walks silently on her other side.

Tiffany is the first to spot the trail markers. The kids heave a collective sigh of relief, which is soon tempered by the realization that the trail is on the opposite side of a ravine that has been carved out by a small stream. The ravine is lined with large glacial boulders and will not be simple to traverse.

"Well guys, what do you think?" asks Dave. "Do you want to try to get across here, or should we walk back along the ravine to where it might not be so steep and rocky?"

Tiffany leads again. "Let's cross here; I don't want to walk all that way back. I want to get to the top of the mountain!"

Once more her determination is infectious, and there are no dissenting votes. All of the kids are able to scramble down and over the stream without too much difficulty. Climbing back up the other incline proves to be another story. The rocks are slippery in places and there is little to grab on to. The more agile and confident climbers make their way fairly easily, with occasional help from Dave and Betsy, but the others are reluctant even to try. Eventually, all except Damian and Larry reach the top of the ravine.

It's the high ropes all over again.

"Come on, Damian and Larry!" encourages Tiffany. "You can do it!"

But Damian is coming unraveled. "I *can't* do it; I can't breathe."

Vanessa shouts back, "If you can't breathe, then how can you be screaming so loud?"

No amount of coaxing budges the two frightened boys. Finally, Dave suggests to Betsy that she go on ahead with the others, and that he will keep working with Larry and Damian and perhaps catch up with the group later.

"Listen, you guys, I know you're scared, and that's okay. But you can do this," he says to the two boys, who are sitting together on a rock, sulking. "All of the others made it up without falling. Besides, either way you look at it, you're going to have to climb out of here."

Both boys look up at the reality of their predicament.

"Now, come on. I'll help you up one at a time," Dave continues.

He reaches out a hand to Larry, who appears to be the less frightened of the two. Ten minutes later, Larry is standing on the top, panting with satisfaction, while Dave goes back for Damian.

"Okay, Damian, it's your turn," says Dave.

"I can't do it, Dave—didn't my mom tell you I have asthma?" Damian lies. "I guess I'll just stay here and die."

"You don't have asthma, and no one's going to die on this trip," returns Dave. "You're just really freaked out, like yesterday when you started out on the high ropes."

Dave pulls Damian to his feet. "You see Larry standing up

there? That's where you're going to be before you know it. Now follow me, and I'll help you when you need it."

Damian loses his nerve several more times on the way up, but each time Dave is able to ease him through his panic. Though it takes him twice as long as Larry, Damian's smile is just as broad when he finally reaches the top.

All goes well until Dave and the boys hit a steep section in the trail, which is beginning to aim earnestly toward the summit. Almost in unison, Larry and Damian whine, "I'm tired. Can we go back?"

"Come on, guys, don't quit on me now," urges Dave. "We've come too far for that." And then, "Do you realize how beautiful it's going to be on top of this mountain? It's so clear today that we'll be able to see all the way to Vermont and maybe even up into New Hampshire."

"I don't care," groans Larry as he sits down in the middle of the trail and lowers his head between his hands. "I just wanna go home."

Out of the corner of his eye Dave spots Damian intentionally tossing his water bottle into the underbrush.

"I have to go back, Dave. I lost my water bottle," Damian declares with a perfectly straight face. "It must've fallen out of my pack."

Time to complete the hike is running out. So is Dave's patience. "Cut it out, Damian. I saw what you just did with your water bottle." He pauses to take a deep breath and collect his thoughts.

"Now, listen," he continues, "I'm going to finish the climb, and I'd like it if you would come with me. Think how good you'll feel when we get to the top."

"I don't want to go. I'm too tired," Larry whines again.

"Me, too," chimes in Damian.

"All right, then," responds Dave, "that's your choice. But listen to me: Stay *right* here and wait for us to pick you up on our way down. You definitely don't want to be lost out in these woods after dark."

Dave waits an interval to give the boys a chance to change their minds. With nothing forthcoming except more sulking, he asks, "Do you promise me you won't move from this spot?"

"Yes."

Dave hurries off without looking back. When he reaches the rocky peak, he finds the others luxuriating in the warm April sunshine. Tiffany's expression is jubilant. Everyone is swept away by the dramatic panorama. Dave informs them that Larry and Damian made it out of the ravine but later chose to stop and go no farther.

"When we meet up with them on the way down," he says, "it's the same rule as yesterday. I don't want to hear anyone putting them down for their decision to stay back."

The group remains on the top of the mountain long enough for Dave to eat the food he's brought and admire the incredible 360-degree view. Anxious about the two boys he left behind, he quickly gathers everyone together and they go bounding down the mountain, with Tiffany, as usual, in the lead.

Before they have gone far Betsy calls out, "Hey, gang, remember what happened this morning! It gets dark real fast up here in the mountains, which means we can't afford to go wandering off the trail again."

Much to Dave's relief, they find Larry and Damian right in the middle of the trail where he left them. The boys have managed to drag an old log over to sit on and are amicably chatting away, laughing occasionally. Dave is staggered by the change in them—especially Damian, who appears almost serene.

The other kids heed Dave's admonition about teasing Larry

and Damian. After a rest, while the two boys drag their seat back off the trail, the reunited troop completes the hike together, arriving back at camp just as daylight is beginning to fade.

The value for children of having the opportunity to take risks and confront their fears, real or imagined, is beyond measure. This is the case with all kids, of course, but it is especially true for vulnerable young people such as Damian and Carl, who carry much more uncertainty inside themselves than others, and who as a result tend to keep their distance. What better way for them to discover inner strength and discipline they didn't know they possessed, to learn that their fears will not consume them?

While the detailed, preestablished structure of the ropes course model is an excellent one because its high level of built-in safety reassures reluctant participants, I think I prefer the kind of improvisational adventure that Betsy, Dave, and the kids had when they climbed Buck Mountain. Here, map and compass—and water bottles—were the only props. The earth, trees, sky, and the individual and collective mettle of the group provided a subtle, open-ended structure that made it possible for each kid to tailor his or her own growth experience. As for Larry and Damian, that they did not make it all the way to the top did not represent failure. Their decision to stop and say "no farther" was fundamentally important, as was their time spent together in the middle of the trail, waiting for the others to return.

I have seen no studies documenting that adventure-based challenge, wild or domestic, has a direct therapeutic effect on distressed children, but my own anecdotal evidence tells me that it most certainly does. The profound calm that settled over Carl, Damian, and Larry after their respective "ordeals" was a sure sign that something in each boy was rearranging itself on a very deep level. Gaps caused by the trauma and chaos of their childhoods were being filled in. Circuits left open by a lifelong deficit of nurturing and bonding were finally being completed. I know that they all returned more whole.

The beauty of the ropes course model is the way in which it combines individual challenge and group cooperation. Each participant is placed in charge of his or her own experience. When kids are given the option of saying "No," as Carl was, they will opt almost every time to push against their fear, to stretch their personal limits. At the same time, the problem-solving initiatives demand that kids work together to find a solution. The group is forced to figure out a way to pull in the kids who might ordinarily find themselves being left out, and the "outcasts" have to be willing to accept the invitation to join the team.

Perhaps most important, the experience is physical. The lessons enter through the body. One of the severest limitations of the conventional educational model is that it addresses children only from the neck up. Except for the token amount of time spent on so-called physical education, the entire emphasis is on the mind. Meanwhile, kids like Damian, Carl, William, Mumasatou, and so many of the millions of Ritalin kids are very physical children. They have a great deal of energy. They need to move about, and to explore and touch and manipulate things.

Thankfully, an increasing number of public schools across the country are building their own ropes courses, realizing that the emotional learning kids accomplish while they are challenging themselves somehow translates into improved learning and behavior in the classroom.

10

Meanwhile, back at school, William has found a home in the art room. One of his first school successes occurred here in the early fall when he wandered into a group of teachers and students busy folding origami peace cranes. The small paper ornaments were for the dedication of a new temple, the Grafton Peace Pagoda, which over a seven-year period many Free Schoolers had helped to build. The pagoda was constructed entirely by volunteers, and our kids spent many hours moving stones, straightening bent nails, and pouring concrete walkways. Jun Yasuda, the diminutive nun from Grafton who belongs to a Japanese Buddhist sect that has built similar shrines to world peace around the globe, had asked area children to create a thousand cranes for the opening ceremony. Folding this number of cranes, she says, is a way of memorializing Sadaka, a young Japanese girl killed by radiation poisoning in the aftermath of the bombing of Hiroshima.

Fashioning a crane out of a four-inch-square piece of paper is no easy task. It requires numerous small folds done in precise order. I would have thought that anyone who told me William possessed the attention span sufficient to do this kind of work was nuts. How wrong William proved me to be. He proceeded to pick up the steps very quickly, and then he spent the following hour making half a dozen well-formed cranes. The accomplishment won him high praise from Colleen, our young art teacher.

Next, William discovered the potter's wheel. These days my wife, Betsy, teaches pottery one day a week at the school, and William has become one of her regulars. Clay is the perfect medium for a boy like him. It's messy, gooey, and very forgiving. The rhythmic rotation of the wheel adds a magical dimension that usually keeps William entranced for hours at a time. Betsy is careful to give him instruction only when he asks for it, which isn't very often. Content simply to squeeze the soft, wet, twirling clay and watch it change shape as it rotates round and round, he cares little when his uncentered creations fall in on themselves because he has worked the wheel at too high a speed and thinned out the walls of his pot too much. William has yet to actually complete a single piece of pottery, but still he returns every week to spin another lump of reddish brown earth between his hands.

Today William's dad comes in to pick William up at three o'clock. William Senior is between jobs right now, so we have been seeing more of him lately. William Junior is still in the art room with Betsy, tidying up after another busy afternoon at the wheel. Despite wearing both an apron and a smock—William has already reported to Betsy that his mother gets mad at him when he comes home dirty—William has managed to get clay on the cuffs of his jeans and his shoes. His father makes no effort to conceal his displeasure.

"Boy, didn't your mother tell you to stop messing up your clothes," William Senior says sternly. "And look at those damn shoes I just bought you."

Then he grabs his son abruptly by the arm and barks, "Now get your coat and let's go."

Betsy immediately drops what she's doing to intervene. "Hi,

I'm Betsy. I don't think we've met," she says, smiling and extending her right hand.

William Senior has to let go of his grip on William Junior in order to shake Betsy's hand.

"I've done everything I can think of to keep William clean in here," Betsy continues. "But, you know, pottery is a lot like playing in the mud, and it's almost impossible for kids not to get a little on them."

"I understand what you're saying. But *you* have to understand that we paid sixty dollars for those sneakers, and I just can't go out and buy him another pair," William Senior returns, trying to quell his rising temper.

Betsy pauses for a moment and then suggests, "We have some waterproof boots in the supply closet; how would it be if he puts a pair of those on when he works at the wheel?"

"All right," answers William Senior, beginning to relax a little. "And why don't I send in an old pair of pants for him to wear."

"That's a great idea," Betsy says, relieved. "You know, William has a real feeling for pottery, and I think the work he's doing in here is very important. I would like to see him continue."

William Junior, who has been intently studying the interaction between these two powerful people, looks relieved, too.

Here I'm reminded of a young British-trained teacher, Sylvia Ashton-Warner, who, on her first assignment, found herself confronted by a roomful of fractious, rebellious Maori children in New Zealand, who weren't about to submit to her classroom routines. Instead, they spent the day laying waste to the contents of the room and to each other.

In her book *Teacher,* Ashton-Warner described the miraculous transformation that took place in her one-room village schoolhouse once she decided to chuck the textbooks and worksheets and all the rest of the standardized methods by which the New Zealand government expected her to operate.[1] As soon as she put away the conventional materials and replaced them with easels, paints, clay, and musical instruments, the fighting ceased. A peaceful, albeit noisy and chaotic, calm settled over the room.

And still the children learned to read and write—not with basal readers and handwriting primers, but with books of their own that they wrote and illustrated. Ashton-Warner found that when the reading vocabulary consisted of meaningful, vivid language that the children generated themselves, they remembered every word. Perhaps her most brilliant insight was this: Every child has a creative "vent" and a destructive one. If the creative vent is not sufficiently open, then a child's energy will flow out of the destructive vent instead. At any given moment, it's going to be one or the other.

Sadly, here in the United States, time for creative expression is continually being squeezed out of the conventional classroom day. The growing obsession with left-brained academics is forcing more and more right-brained activities such as art, music, dance, and drama into after-school time slots, if they aren't eliminated altogether. Oftentimes, the kids who need them the most are the least likely to have access to them.

Apparently there were no repercussions from William Senior's face-off with Betsy in the art room, because he came in the next morning and volunteered to conduct a basketball clinic for the kids. Still out of work, he says he has plenty of time on his hands. It turns out that he played basketball against Michael

Jordan in high school, and then went on to an impressive college career.

William Junior has been beside himself while waiting for his dad to arrive for the clinic. I lost count of how many times he asked me, "When's my daddy coming? When's my daddy coming?"

As soon as William Senior shows up, we troop around the corner to the neighborhood settlement house that generously allows us to use their gym in the afternoons.

William Senior, now Coach William, is a towering presence in the small turn-of-the-century gymnasium. He proceeds to run the kids through an hour-long series of dribbling, passing, and shooting drills, followed by a scrimmage between two hastily arranged teams. William Junior does an impressive job of not demanding too much special attention from his father, who has his hands full dealing with the group's wide range of skill levels.

When the game is over, Coach William gathers the tired yet still excited participants in a circle at mid-court to review the day's lessons and answer questions. The kids are all dying to hear about what it was like to play against Michael Jordan. Wistfully, Coach William recounts the story of the high school state championship game in which he and Jordan were the senior captains on opposing teams. He tells the kids that he actually outscored the king of basketball and led his team to victory in that climactic contest, but that it was Michael Jordan who would go on to stardom in college and then an unprecedented professional career.

Without the kids' realizing it, Coach William is easing into the kind of motivational talk that is a feature of youth basketball clinics.

"We all make mistakes in life," he says, his expression turning regretful. "And I made certain mistakes along the way that Michael Jordan was wise enough not to make. That's why he's where he is and I'm where I am today."

With the average age of the clinic only around eight or nine, Coach William elects not to flesh out the details of his "mistakes." The kids don't ask him to elaborate. He ends his impromptu sermon by telling them that the most important thing in life is to be willing to admit when you are on the wrong track, and then to do your best to get back on the right one again.

"That's all anyone can ask of you," he concludes. Then, "Hey, you kids were great today. Thanks for inviting me."

The kids clearly have been captivated by their coach's earnestness. They respond with applause and a chorus of thank-yous. But what caught my attention most was how William Junior's focus remained riveted on his dad throughout his talk. William Junior sat right next to his father, and, judging by the look on William Junior's face, a mixture of love, pride, and intense admiration, it is obvious that he internalized every word. All of the kids were enriched by William Senior's clinic, but none more than his young son, whose self-image and connection to his father have just received an important, much-needed boost.

William is what many psychologists would call an "unbonded" child. Unbonded children lack a natural sense of attachment and relatedness to others. They persistently fail to consider the effects of their actions. They are reluctant to give up the infantile perception that they are the center of the universe. They are often hostile and aggressive, and lack compassion.

The overwhelming majority of the Free School's Ritalin kids

over the years have exhibited a disconnectedness similar to William's. In no instance did we have the sense that being unbonded was a genetic condition. In nearly every instance there were obvious fractures in the family. Fathers were often absent. Even in William's case, where his parents are still together, his bond to his father is shaky because his father is away for long periods, leaving his mother to perform the bulk of the parenting.

Healthy bonding starts in the moments after birth. According to the educator Joseph Chilton Pearce, two major disrupters of bonding are modern, medicalized childbirth practices and the absence of breastfeeding.[2] During an overwhelming majority of *normal* hospital births, says Pearce, the routine technological interventions and institutional protocols serve to disrupt the deep levels of bonding between mother (and father) and baby that nature intends for all mammalian life.

The bonding process begins in earnest when the mother draws her newborn to her breast. The skin-to-skin and eye contact that occur between mother and baby activate within the infant a series of profound neurological and psychological processes, some of which have a window of opportunity only during the first twenty-four hours. At the same time, however, standard operating procedure on a modern maternity ward calls for the baby to be taken from its mother right after he or she lands in the obstetrician's rubber-gloved hands and is turned over to a nurse for washing, weighing, and a set of invasive, painful procedures aimed at preventing certain one-in-a-million infant diseases.

In addition, continues Pearce, breastfeeding has been so discouraged by the medical establishment during the twentieth century that by the 1950s, 96 percent of American mothers were no longer doing it. This figure has dropped somewhat in the past four decades due to consumer pressure from the natural childbirth movement, but the figure is still alarmingly high.

William was born in a large New York City hospital where health care for the poor, especially the minority poor, is notoriously substandard. Well-insured middle class patrons often use cozy birthing suites with rooming-in privileges for the baby, while the poor get the cold, harsh, brightly lit, surgical bed delivery room. Their babies spend the majority of the next forty-eight to seventy-two hours in a crowded nursery where they are rarely held or touched by anyone. There is no one to advise unwitting mothers about the positive developmental benefits of breastfeeding. As a result, William and his brother were both bottle-fed babies.

Thankfully, damaged bonding can be reversed. To this end we make the fostering of relatedness a major goal at the Free School. It is a primary reason why the school is a community, and why we place so much emphasis on relationships. It's why learning is a cooperative rather than a competitive endeavor here. It's also why we encourage parents to participate in the life of the school. The value to William of his father's time spent with him and his classmates cannot be overstated. Strengthening William's experience of the connection between home and school will go a long way toward helping him to become more sociable, and this in turn will help him to settle down, focus, and grow more competent in cognitive areas as well.

Yesterday Brian stayed home from school so that he and his mother's boyfriend, Jim, could cruise around and pick up the food donations for tomorrow night's French dinner. The other kids in the class spent the day busily making preparations with our teacher Jeff, who is a former chef and has volunteered to help cook with Jim. It is shaping up to be one of the most elaborate fundraising dinners ever. Tomorrow—Saturday—a bevy of volunteers will pitch in to convert the entire upstairs big room into a proper restaurant. I have arranged to borrow tables and chairs from a nearby church, and through an old connection Jeff has gotten free table linens and uniforms for the night. There will be candlelit tables and French music playing in the background. The three girls in the class have designed a beautiful bilingual menu, and all of the kids will serve as waiters and waitresses, smartly dressed in their white uniforms.

Lex and the kids have been publicizing the dinner all over town, and they are hoping for a big turnout. In fact, they are counting on a big turnout, because they are still over a thousand dollars shy of their trip budget and they are scheduled to board the train for Colorado on Tuesday.

On Saturday the school fills with exotic aromas. Brian has asked to be the chef's assistant, and his classmates have all agreed. He looks very professional in his full-length white apron and tall white hat. His fast-paced energy is a perfect match for the intense pulse of a restaurant kitchen.

While Brian is in the kitchen prepping a mountain of donated vegetables for soup and salad for at least a hundred guests, the rest of the class and a half-dozen volunteers are out performing miracles in the big room. They have removed the climbing structure and the block corner walls, and packed up all the toys and stored them in the kindergarten room. Nancy has brought in an assortment of batik fabrics to hang on the walls, and three floor lamps will shed a softer light than the overhead fluorescents.

It takes several attempts before the tables and chairs are arranged in such a way that they will seat a hundred diners and still allow enough space for the waiters and waitresses to move about. By the time the first guest arrives a little before six, the transformation is complete. Each linen-covered table has a small vase of flowers in the center and a lit taper at either end, and each place is set with a white linen napkin and the correct silverware. Thanks to audiotapes brought in by the mother of Michel, the little boy that Mumasatou "adopted" several years ago and who is still in the school, the French singer Edith Piaf is singing mournfully in the background. Soon the collective noise of the crowd will drown her out, but in the beginning the effect is quite dramatic. How would guests know that they weren't dining in one of the finest restaurants in Paris?

The room fills quickly, and the kids are hard pressed to keep up. Jim and Jeff's extensive experience keeps panic from setting in and the food flowing smoothly from the kitchen out to the big room. In the meantime, Brian's entire family has arrived, enough parents, grandparents, aunts, uncles, and cousins to fill a table for ten. By six-forty-five nearly every seat in the house is filled, and there is some concern over the supply of food if guests continue to arrive at the rate they have been.

Fortunately, the food holds out, and at seven-thirty the majority of the crowd has finished eating and is beginning to clamor for dessert. This means it's time for one of the school's infamous cake auctions. The seventh and eighth graders have solicited at least twenty cakes and pies from parents and other supporters in the community for part two of their fundraising evening. My bullhorn voice seems to have earned me the permanent role of auctioneer. My job: to make sure no one goes home with any money left in his or her pockets.

But first I run through all of the thank-yous and acknowledgments of businesses and individuals that made tonight possible. I save for last the two chefs and their young assistant, who are still working back in the kitchen. When I call them out and introduce them, the crowd bursts into a rousing ovation. As well they should, for they have just eaten a meal that would have cost them dearly at any of the French restaurants in town. Brian, standing between Jim and Jeff, is absolutely beaming. And so is everyone at his family table.

Cake auctions are raucous affairs. Competition for coveted items can be fierce, with as many as a dozen people vying to be the highest bidders. Kids sit next to their parents, pleading with them to raise their hands again and stay in the race. Tonight a chocolate mousse cake by a young mother who once baked professionally fetches more than fifty dollars. A French-style cheesecake made by Michel's mom nets almost forty.

When the last dessert has been sold and the winning bids tallied, the cake monies total over four hundred dollars. After the class treasurer adds in the proceeds from the dinner and the additional raffle tickets sold at the door, the profit for the evening comes to more than $1,300.

Part three of tonight's event is the drawing for the thirty or so prizes that the kids solicited. This takes another half-hour, followed by two hours of kitchen cleanup and restoring the big room to its former status. By the time the last borrowed table and chair are loaded into the school van so they can be returned to the church tomorrow, it is approaching eleven p.m. The seven seventh and eighth graders—Tyrone mysteriously failed to show up tonight—head for home exhausted from their twelve-hour day. But far more dominant are the feelings of relief and satisfaction that come from knowing that they have raised more than enough cash for their big trip.

On Monday morning the class asks Tyrone about his absence Saturday night, and by way of a response he finally declares he won't be going to Colorado because then he would have to miss a couple of games in the spring basketball league he has joined. Everyone in the group silently senses the real reason why he is backing out—he's too afraid to be away from home for so long—and elects to take his reasoning at face value. In many ways, Tyrone's pride is all he has to see him through during the rest of his adolescence.

Brian, meanwhile, has a problem of a different sort. The girls are still angry that he and Tyrone were always goofing off while they were out selling raffle tickets and magazine ads, regardless of the key role Brian played in pulling off the French dinner. The girls refuse to give ground on the agreement that everyone has to sell his or her share in order to go on the trip. Rightly so, Lex backs them up completely.

This leaves Brian in a real bind. His charm and pleas for mercy get him nowhere, as does his argument that the class already has more than enough money. And now he has only two days left to raise an additional $110. To add to his troubles, the raffle is over, meaning that the only remaining option is to sell more ads for the magazine, which the class will publish and distribute when they return from Colorado.

Word of Brian's predicament somehow reaches me. Knowing how badly he wants to go on the trip and how hard he did work at times, I decide to come to his rescue. I offer to take him downtown to some of the stores and businesses that his classmates missed while Lex and the others go buy food and other necessities for the train ride. He gratefully and wisely accepts.

Brian is glad to be in a situation where his charm is an asset again. He turns it on full power and in less than two hours he sells four ads and has $120 safely tucked away in his folder. We get back to school well ahead of the others, who are still out shopping.

Helping Brian to complete his share of the work for the class trip is a perfect example of what educator Alfie Kohn writes about in his book *Punished by Rewards*. According to Kohn, children perform far better and learn far more when their motivation comes from within themselves.[3] The author, who has most recently become an outspoken critic of the standardized testing movement, begins by reexamining the work of B. F. Skinner. Skinner was the inventor of behavior modification, the psychology on which the carrot-and-stick approach to education practiced by the overwhelming majority of schools is constructed. Behavior modification is based on the simple principle that a particular behavior is more likely to be repeated if it is immediately followed by a reward, or "reinforcement."

Skinner's behavioral theory, developed in the 1930s, was based solely on experiments conducted with rats and pigeons. His lab rats would persistently figure out how to run the maze regardless of the number of obstacles he placed in their way, as long as that piece of cheese was always waiting for them at the end. But more recently, Kohn points out, social psychologists have conducted scores of behavioral experiments involving humans that have all produced the opposite result; namely that the more people are rewarded for doing something, the more they lose interest in whatever they had to accomplish to get the reward. For example, research shows that students who are given grades and rewarded with A's become less motivated to learn than those who are given no grades at all.

The only thing carrots and sticks in school really produce, says Kohn, is temporary compliance. They reduce students' sense of the value of what they're doing. In fact, even as mild a form of positive reinforcement as praise can significantly inhibit learning because it fosters dependency in the learner. When there's no one around to do the praising, the learner suddenly feels no motivation to learn. The only true motivation, Kohn concludes, is self-motivation. I couldn't agree more.

The one addition I would make to the issues Kohn is raising, which apply to every type of child—and equally to adults, for that matter—is that they especially apply to Ritalin kids. What Ritalin kids need are real, here-and-now incentives to achieve, not the present threats and future promises that propel the academic agenda of the conventional school model. They need the space to discover their own intrinsic reasons for developing the skills and the knowledge they will need in order to lead satisfying adult lives, as well as for confronting their dysfunctional patterns and runaway impulses.

Brian's class trip is a perfect example of how so much of the important learning is structured at the Free School. The kids will have to utilize all of their basic skills in order to carry out the necessary planning and fundraising—for a project that is entirely of their own design. Planning the itinerary, which is the students' responsibility, involves a lot of careful reading. The magazine, one of their major fundraising activities, will require high-quality writing, as well as careful editing and proofreading. High-level computer skills will be required for the typesetting, graphics, and layout. The budgeting of travel expenses and the bookkeeping associated with fundraising involves plenty of math. And perhaps most important, in Brian's case he has ample motivation to practice the self-control that will enable him to get his share of the work done.

Meanwhile, William has seemed more on edge lately. He's been involved in several fights in school and is becoming defiant again whenever anyone tries to set limits with him. We have been assuming that the regression has a lot to do, as in Damian's case, with his mother's rapidly advancing pregnancy. But this morning, William shares with me in a hushed tone that his mom and dad had a big fight the other night. His dad, he says, has moved out for good. Interestingly, just yesterday William's mother, Irene, informed us that William Senior has gotten a long-distance truck-driving job that will require him to spend the next month in North Carolina so that he can get the necessary training to update his driver's license. The week before, however, William Senior told me when he came in to pick up William Junior that he had landed a local short-haul job that would enable him to be home by five, thus giving him more time to spend with his boys.

My intuition tells me that William Junior's story is probably the more accurate one. In any event, William's dad is gone, at least for now. His absence comes at a time when there is already a lot of family stress. Irene has been suffering increasingly severe lower back pain, and the combination of both parents' being out of work and a newly rented, more expensive uptown apartment is causing serious financial difficulties. Also, Irene recently confided to Nancy that she is tired of being pregnant, and that she was deeply disappointed when she found out the new baby is going to be a boy.

"I wanted a girl so bad," she said, gesturing toward the top of her forehead. "I've had it up to here with raising boys."

Unfortunately, William's behavior in council meetings is deteriorating again, too. He's been dutifully showing up for meetings, then quickly making everyone wish he hadn't. Given the circumstances, we do our best to be tolerant. William, meanwhile, is busy practicing the entire repertoire of disruption techniques he mastered last year in kindergarten. He finally goes too far and the chairperson sends him to sit on a folding chair in the kitchen until the meeting is over.

William's transgression, of course, means yet another loss of swimming privileges. When swimming day rolls around, William again raises no fuss about having to remain outside the pool. This time I suggest to him that he bring along something to do for the hour, a book, or a game, or some drawing supplies, but he pretends not to hear me and trudges despondently out to the van, empty-handed.

Once at the public pool, William makes no attempt to attract my negative attention. After chatting amicably with me for a while on the bench, he begins pacing around the pool in hopes of engaging the others in play, today with some success. He eventually manages to tempt his classmates in the shallow end into splashing him. Dodging nearly all of the water launched at him from the pool, William seems to have no interest in getting wet today.

When the others grow tired of the game and return to their swimming, William sidles back over toward me, looking bored. I decide to see if I can engage him in a conversation about his present predicament.

"You hate missing out on swimming, don't you?" I ask.

"Yeah."

"Then why do you keep getting yourself in trouble in council meetings?"

"Because council meetings are stupid," he answers. "They're so boring."

"You know, a lot of kids feel that way," I return. "And so do I sometimes. But we couldn't have a peaceful school without council meetings."

I recount the story of the time six-year-old Nicky managed to get mandatory attendance at council meetings voted out and how disastrous it was for everyone.

"So there has to be some way to make sure kids take council meetings seriously," I continue. "Since you hate missing swimming so much, do you have any other ideas for a consequence when the chairperson has to kick you out of a council meeting?"

His reply is like a reflex. "Put me on punishment."

I ask him what he means by this. He says it's what his parents do at home whenever he's "bad."

I am struck by William's quick use of the sentence "Put me on punishment." It appears that being punished has already become a well-worn path in his life. I repeat my question about whether he can think of a different consequence for when he disrupts council meetings. He pauses for several moments, his face scrunched up to aid his thought process, and then shakes his head "No" with a certain finality.

"Well," I say, "why don't you keep thinking about it, and let me know if you come up with something. I would be willing to make a new motion at the next council meeting."

Yes, William still disrupts council meetings on occasion, but he has come a long way since September. I'm particularly pleased by the progression of his reactions to the limits we have set for him. The first time we stopped him he threw a raging fit and tried to make himself larger than the limits. He tested them outrageously the second time, going so far as to enter the pool with his shoes on in an attempt to provoke a reaction from me. Here, perhaps, he was attempting to get me to feel his anger for him. Had I gotten mad, he would have had permission to burst out with his own wounded feelings. This kind of emotional confusion is not uncommon between parents and their children. Because I'm not William's father, I was able to muster enough patience and perspective to see what William was up to and prevent him from manipulating me. If I had let William provoke me to anger, or if I had given him justification to get mad by intervening, he would have had me right where he wanted—playing *his* game. Instead, when William got virtually no reaction from me, even though he had climbed into the pool in his sneakers, he gave up his testing and moved on.

The third time around William began to accept the consequence, not like a chastised dog with his tail between his legs, but with a certain matter-of-factness. It was fine to let him make the best of the situation and have a little fun. The idea, after all, wasn't to punish him, but rather to help him learn new behaviors. As soon as I saw that he had ceased trying to rise above the limits, I decided to include him in the process by asking him to suggest an alternative consequence, which unfortunately he was unable to do. This is a very effective way of encouraging kids to take responsibility for their misbehavior and often speeds up the process of transformation. However, in William's case, he's already been punished so much that he's like an old vinyl record that has developed a deep groove in which the needle keeps getting stuck. Now he needs a little bump to unstick himself—though not so hard a bump that he gets scratched.

Children like William *are* capable of changing basic patterns of thought, attitude, and behavior. But it takes time. Old habits are hard to break. Still, William is only six. His basic character and personality are still quite malleable. And yet this is exactly the age when our educational system begins to bear down on children. They are quickly slotted into categories of behavioral or cognitive pathology from which few ever escape. Moreover, the drugs that are administered to them preclude them from ever doing real repair to their beings—assuming any is needed in the first place. At the risk of sounding like a broken record myself, Ritalin and the other drugs merely smooth over so-called symptoms. They make the kids "functional," less of a bother. They do nothing to address the causes of childhood distress or to support real healing.

11

It hardly seems possible that two weeks have passed since Brian and his classmates left for Colorado. They return triumphant, having had quite an adventure. Through the frequent bizarreness of fate, they ended up arriving at the Jefferson County Open School, the public alternative school just outside Denver where they had been invited to spend the day and night, only an hour before the killing spree began at Columbine High School —located just four miles down the same highway. Our kids could hear the police and media helicopters as they hovered over the scene of the tragedy, and they watched the disturbing developments unfold on an old television set that the physical education teacher had turned on in the gym.

During the course of the day, Brian, who makes new friends easily, got to know several students who had friends at Columbine. By three o'clock, a hushed and somber cloud had settled over everyone. Because of official fears that someone may have also planted bombs in Jefferson County Open, the Free Schoolers were asked to be packed up and ready to leave the following morning at six, so that bomb-sniffing dogs could make a sweep through the building.

A Jefferson County Open teacher generously volunteered to drive Lex and the kids up into the mountains to the conference. Snow began falling almost immediately upon their arrival at the site, and by the time the storm ended three days later, the walkways between cabins were more like tunnels. The seventy-five or so young people in attendance, some from snow-free climates, were in seventh heaven.

On their homeward journey, the group stopped in Chicago, as planned, for a three-day tour of the city. They were hosted by the Pedro Albizu Campos School, an inner-city Puerto Rican alternative school that had sent a delegation to the Colorado conference. Again it was the affable, outgoing Brian who repeatedly found ways to break the ice between the two groups of young people from very different cultures.

Back at school on Monday, Brian tries to revive Tyrone's fallen spirits. Before the trip, in an effort to get Tyrone to change his mind, I had done my best to help him visualize how left out he was likely to feel when the others returned so full of stories. How right I proved to be. The normally boisterous, wisecracking fourteen-year-old is strangely quiet. In the afternoon, Brian, who is much more bonded to the rest of the class than he was before the trip, breaks away from the group and urges Tyrone up to the basketball court for a game of one-on-one. He also invites Tyrone to spend the weekend at his house. By Friday, Tyrone, while still sporting a sober look rarely seen in the past, is more or less back to his old self.

While the seventh and eighth graders were away, Damian got his wish. In early May, his mother gave birth to a beautiful baby girl. Paula reports that Damian's behavior has improved again at home. She says that he's being helpful around the house and gentle and nurturing with his new sister.

We're seeing a similar improvement in Damian at school. His defiance has subsided considerably, and he's spending less time around the little kids. Lately, he has been working on a play that he plans to premiere at the annual end-of-the-school-year talent show. With the script he's been writing with Andrew nearly completed, he has started building elaborate stage sets out of large cardboard boxes.

Nancy and I decide it's time to ask Paula whether or not Damian will be returning to the Free School next September. While all of the signals from her have been positive thus far, Damian hasn't done a whole lot of conventional schoolwork this year.

Paula's answer is unequivocal: "I wouldn't dream of sending him anywhere else. I can't believe how much he has improved in only seven months."

Then as an afterthought, "I'm only sorry I didn't find you sooner."

William comes in one morning with a shiny new asthma inhaler. This prompts an immediate phone call to Irene, who informs Nancy that when she noticed William wheezing in his sleep over the weekend, she took him to the emergency room. The physician who examined William diagnosed him with asthma and gave Irene a prescription for the inhaler.

Nancy explains that we don't like to encourage the use of these powerful asthma medications unless absolutely necessary, and that we would prefer to hold on to the inhaler for William and watch him carefully for the next several days. Nancy reassures Irene by describing how kids seldom suffer asthma symptoms in our school because of the high level of physical activity and emotional freedom. She says that William is probably reacting to the pending arrival of the new baby and William Senior's absence, and that she doubts William is developing full-blown asthma.

Thanks to the friendly rapport Nancy and Irene have developed over the course of the school year, Irene readily accepts Nancy's assessment of the situation, which would later prove to be entirely accurate.

Brian, too, starts regressing once he settles back into school and renews his relationship with Tyrone, repeating the disruptive behaviors that marked his arrival two years ago. He is always clowning around in the editorial meetings of the class magazine, and Lex and the girls have to nag him constantly to get him to do any of the work.

When Lex comes to me for advice, I suggest that he minimize the amount of time Brian has to spend in meetings and instead assign him specific tasks and insist that he complete them.

"My guess is that he is pretty freaked out at the thought of leaving us for public school next year," I say to Lex. "We haven't exactly worked any academic miracles with him."

Then, still thinking out loud, "And maybe he is still feeling the effects of being so close to the Columbine massacre. It touched him very deeply, I think. How would it be if I came in and talked with your kids about their experience?"

Lex and I make arrangements for me to visit his class first thing the next morning.

Before Lex leaves, I also suggest to him that it might be a good idea to help Brian come up with an end-of-the-year project, something physically engaging that will drain off some of his anxiety.

"It's crucial that his time with us end on a positive note," I reflect, "because I think we can assume that his transition into high school isn't going to be an easy one."

"Come to think of it, Brian really got into drumming with the Puerto Rican kids in Chicago," Lex says to me. "And I have a drum maker friend who likes kids a lot. I bet if I asked him to help Brian make a drum, he would do it."

"That sounds absolutely perfect," I reply.

The following day I come in at the end of the seventh and eighth graders' morning meeting and ask if they would be up for sharing some more of their thoughts and feelings about the shootings at Columbine. The topic has been on the minds of teachers, students, and parents all across America.

Brian is the first to speak up. He wistfully talks about some of the friends he made that day at Jefferson County Open who were worried about students they knew at Columbine. All, in turn, express how horrified they still are at the thought of young people killing other young people in cold blood.

When I ask the class what they think some of the causes of the tragedy might be, there is no shortage of ideas: the easy availability of guns, teasing and bullying and being left out, cliques, parents who don't pay enough attention to their kids. Then several kids in succession pick up how the perpetrators had been trapped in a school where no one talks about their feelings and people don't work out their problems with one another. The anger festered inside the two boys until one day they just snapped.

I have little to add to the group's analysis. Lex, however, has waited patiently for the kids to complete their thoughts before adding one little-publicized fact: both of the boys were taking biopsychiatric drugs.

As Irene's due date approaches, William's behavior is deteriorating further, just as Damian's did the closer his mother came to giving birth. William seems determined to get us to send him home, which, in the end, has been the only alternative consequence he has been able to come up with for his council meeting misbehavior. It doesn't surprise me in the least that, with the appearance of his rival imminent, William wants to be by his mother's side night and day. I make it clear to William that being sent home is not an option, that if necessary he will just continue to miss out on swimming.

William and his mother continue to tell different stories about William Senior. Now William is saying that his dad is never coming back, while Irene maintains that her husband will return as soon as he gets his new truck-driving license.

Then, three days after the baby is born, William Senior drives up from North Carolina, spends a long weekend with the family, and leaves again, this time for good.

William comes into school the following Monday proudly showing off a Polaroid photo of his new brother. The resemblance is striking. So is the change in William. He is less volatile and no longer as tense or angry-looking. But his excitement about the baby is tinged with a heavy air of sadness over the departure of his dad. William cries openly when he talks about how much he misses him. In return he receives many sympathetic responses from fellow students and teachers alike.

The remainder of William's school year is largely uneventful. He manages to keep himself within tolerable limits in council meetings, faithfully attends Betsy's weekly pottery sessions, and by June can be found spending progressively longer periods doing projects with Nancy and the rest of her first-graders. The warm weather causes a severe outbreak of baseball fever, with William among the group of mostly older kids who play practically every nonrainy afternoon. William has exceptional skills for a boy his age, but what impresses me most is his ability to play cooperatively enough to stay in the games. This would not have been possible in the fall, when he was too temperamental and self-centered to engage in team sports for any sustained length of time.

All might be said to be going well, except for one thing: William is still not reading. Furthermore, he continues to show scant interest in learning how. On rare occasions, Nancy or I have been able to coax him into being read to, but that's about it. While neither of us is particularly worried, because we are confident that he will learn to read with relative ease once he's ready and decides to invest himself in the process, his mother has reached the alarmed stage. Nancy's and my reassuring words no longer seem to have much effect. As far as Irene is concerned, her son is nearly in the second grade and is falling further and further behind the rest of the nation's children every day.

Irene's fear is understandable. Education rhetoric and public policy keep calling for the earlier mastery of basic skills. And perhaps minority families, who widely perceive educational achievement to be the way out of poverty, feel the pressure for early school success most acutely. Given the economic prejudice young African-American males face in this country, I find it difficult to argue with this point of view.

Unlike William, Mark is learning to read. At his own choosing, he continues his daily thirty- to forty-five-minute reading lessons with Nancy. He is making consistent progress and seems unfettered with any notion that he should be reading better than he is. It makes such a difference that no one is pressuring him or attaching value to his being ten years old and not yet a fluent reader.

Far more important, Mark seems happy with himself and

his world. At this point he has developed several close friendships with other boys in the school. He is frequently elected to
chair council meetings not on the basis of popularity—though
he is very popular—but because he runs the meetings deftly,
always with a touch of humor, and because others sense how
much he genuinely cares about the school.

There are many examples of his caring. Just last week, when
someone sat down too hard on the piano bench and broke one
of the legs, it was Mark—who doesn't even play the piano—who
offered to spend the afternoon helping me fix it. It is also Mark
who very often volunteers to do the phoning or letter writing
involved in arranging field trips and special activities.

Mark is such a pleasure to be with. He is respectful and
responsible, and exceedingly honest. He speaks his mind freely
and doesn't try to hide his feelings. I can only think that he is
going to make a fine man one day and live the life he chooses to
live.

Walter, meanwhile, is loving every minute of his web site design
apprenticeship. He eagerly heads off with Jeff every Thursday to
spend the afternoon working alongside Jodie in her office. Walter may well be the youngest Free School student ever to do an
apprenticeship, and yet he is getting as much or more out of it
than any kid I've seen. Just the other day he announced that he
wants to start a small business for retailing video games, for
which he would develop his own web site to do the marketing.
He has been surfing various government web sites and downloading the necessary forms so that he can operate legally.
Apparently his grandmother has offered to loan him the
twenty-five dollars it will cost to file his as yet undetermined
company name with the county clerk's office.

So here is Walter, more independent than ever, steadily inventing the world in which he wants to live. Walter didn't need a powerful neurostimulant to suppress his imagination and will and to enhance the ability of the left hemisphere of his neocortex to narrow down its focus—two of the effects that Ritalin and the other stimulant drugs have on most children. No, what he needs is an environment that trusts him to know what's best for him, that allows him to follow his own inner guidance. The curriculum Walter is creating may not be the right one for anyone else on the planet, but it is the perfect one for him.

Quite frankly, it is hard to picture anyone ever having viewed Walter as a problem student. He is busy learning every day here. In all his years with us, I don't think he has ever bothered anyone. He treats others the way he wants to be treated, and as a result he has many friends. Even though he has always spent countless hours doing his own thing, we have never had to worry about where he is or what he is up to, because he is always a responsible member of the community.

Which isn't to say that we aren't concerned about Walter from time to time. Our concerns, however, have to do with Walter's emotional and physical well-being. Walter's household is frequently in crisis. His emotional needs sometimes go ignored for long periods of time. As a result, he has learned to substitute food for loving attention, and at this point he is significantly overweight. It is a condition that may well tax his health as he grows older.

The good news is that no one in our school ever teases Walter about his weight. I sincerely doubt this would be the case were he still in public school, where kids, especially as they grow older, can be merciless in taking their pent-up frustrations out on one another. It's not to say that Free School students don't tease one another on occasion—teasing is a natural child behavior the world over. But Free Schoolers indulge in a lot less of it, I think, because their every movement isn't scrutinized, their every act isn't measured and judged. Moreover, they associate with one another on their own terms, and they lean heavily on their classmates to keep the peace in the school.

Which leaves Walter free to go on being Walter.

We learn from Tanya's mother that she and Lamar have split up. Missy has been hearing from both partners that they have been fighting lately, but the announcement still comes as a bit of a shock. Marta and Lamar have decided to split up responsibility for the children as well. Tanya will remain living with her mother, while Tanya's little brother, Beejay, has gone to live with Lamar at Lamar's mother's house.

There is more news: Marta has gotten a job promotion and can now afford to move to the suburbs. After a lifetime in the inner city, she is anxious to leave the noise and turmoil behind her. Her new apartment is in one of the better school districts in the area, and she has decided that in September she will enroll Tanya in first grade at the local elementary school.

I almost wish there were a reason to try to persuade Marta to keep her daughter with us, but there isn't. Tanya is doing beautifully in Missy's kindergarten class. She loves to read and write and is making excellent progress. Also, she's no longer so willful and hungry for attention that she can't function as part of a group. Missy says that Tanya is very cooperative now, and quite teachable.

No, Tanya will probably have no trouble making the transition into public school. But I, for one, will miss her feisty presence and will regret not getting to watch up close the development of the child of a man who was once my student.

*   *   *

Meanwhile, Brian jumped at the idea of building a drum when Lex proposed it, and Lex succeeds in hooking Brian up with his drum-making friend. Dan, a carpenter by trade, has spent a considerable amount of time on a Native American reservation, where he learned how to make wooden drums with deerskin and sinew heads. Dan strikes a deal with Brian: He will teach Brian how to make a drum if Brian will scrape enough deer hide for Dan so he can make a new drum, too. One of Dan's hunting friends has donated a hide for the project, which Dan has already soaked in salt water to loosen the hair and fat that must be removed from both sides.

Still, scraping the hide will be tedious, physical work—just the right medicine for an impatient boy who is worried about his future. After Dan and Brian construct a wooden frame and stretch out the hide on it, Dan shows Brian how to use a small steel scraper to prepare the hide. He cautions him against scraping too hard, or else he will rip through the hide and render it useless as a drumskin. Once the master is satisfied that his apprentice has the right feel for the process, he returns to the house he is helping to build and tells Brian to call him when the hide is ready.

Lex has also successfully helped Brian negotiate an agreement with the girls in the class, who have taken on the role of editing their magazine, whereby they will excuse Brian from the magazine sessions as long as he completes on time the travel journal that he has agreed to write for it.

The drum project is a true test for Brian. He has been spending countless hours scraping the hide—on beautiful spring days when he would much rather be doing other things—and he still has a ways to go on the side with the hair. But despite how tedious and smelly the work is, he continues to scrape. It must be kept in mind here that Brian, an impulsive boy with a long history of not finishing work in his previous schools, is free to drop the project at any time. He won't be graded on it or in any other way penalized by Dan if he doesn't finish. Brian's sole motivation is to build his own drum so that he can continue the drumming that he learned while visiting the *barrio* in Chicago.

Of course the project has another piece of built-in motivation: Brian likes and admires Dan. With Brian's dad largely absent from the scene and his mother's boyfriend, Jim, a relative —and very busy—newcomer in his life, Brian is hungry for male mentoring. He instinctively enjoys being with Dan and wants to show him that he has what it takes to finish a job.

There are afternoons when Brian skips out to play basketball with Tyrone, who finds the deer hide too slimy and gross to want to help his friend. But after a week or so, Brian finally finishes scraping both sides and calls Dan to ask him to come back to teach him how to build the body of the drum.

The next step is fashioning and joining the pieces of birch that will form the body. Using a table saw and planer that a woodworking member of the Free School community has given them permission to use, Dan carefully shows Brian how to cut and smooth the patterned pieces of wood, which they will then notch and glue together. Dan, recognizing that Brian has been influenced by the Puerto Rican style, has helped Brian to design a tallish, conical drum similar to a small conga.

The rest of Brian's class is busy moving the magazine along. They are much better off without his disruptive presence. Brian, in turn, completes his contribution as promised, with Lex's guidance and support. It is a very readable article recounting the highlights of the big trip. Although Brian hasn't done nearly as much work on the magazine as some of his classmates, he can still take pride in its completion.

When the kids finish marketing the finished product—a local copy shop donated the paper and printing—they have more than two hundred dollars in the class treasury. It is enough for one last end-of-the-year hurrah, a whitewater rafting trip. Betsy has a friend who runs a rafting business on the upper Hudson River, and he has offered the group a generous discount.

On the appointed day Betsy is unable to help Lex chaperone the trip, so I arrange to fill in for her. Because our nine-thirty a.m. appointment with the river requires us to leave school at seven, the rare beauty of the morning is a bit lost on us as we sleepily make the hundred-mile drive north in the school van. Having never rafted before—and not being a terribly proficient swimmer, either—I have my mounting excitement to keep me alert behind the wheel.

It's a beautiful sight when I look into the rearview mirror and see Tyrone's heavy-lidded eyes peering out from underneath his dark blue New York Yankees cap. I'm glad he's decided to join his classmates for their final adventure together. He grew very excited when the rafting idea was first proposed and willingly helped with the selling of the magazine. Now he is slumped down next to Brian in the seat behind me, and the two good friends are chatting quietly about nothing in particular.

We stop first at the rafting company equipment shed, where our guide issues everyone wetsuits, life jackets, helmets, and broad, hard plastic paddles. Once outfitted, we are herded onto an old purple school bus with a much larger group, seniors from a nearby rural high school, and driven to the launch site just below the dam on a small lake that feeds into the Hudson.

On the bus the guides join together to give everyone paddling and safety instructions. Rafting is a perfectly safe activity, we are told, because the wetsuits and life jacket will keep us afloat even in the most turbulent water. It is imperative, however, should any of us be ejected from the raft—which apparently occurs with some frequency—that we remember not to try to stand up in the river. We must keep our feet up and let the current carry us down into calmer water, and then wait for the raft to retrieve us. Drowning occurs when people's legs get pinned underneath large rocks and the rushing water forces their head underneath the surface.

Everyone is buzzing as we board the raft. Our guide explains that the closer one sits to the front, the wilder the ride will be. Predictably, Brian and Tyrone rush forward, and there is little argument from the others. After the warning about getting stuck under rocks in the middle of the rapids, everyone else, I suspect, has a profound interest in remaining in the boat.

The ride is deceptively calm at first. The dam has released a large quantity of water and we are riding its surge down a small tributary. After a mile or so, the view widens and suddenly we find ourselves in the middle of the Hudson, which is about a hundred yards across here in its northern reaches.

"This is the same river that flows past New York City and out into the Atlantic Ocean," I point out, clinging to my identity as a teacher. "Down there the Hudson is nearly a mile wide."

"Hey, where are the rapids?" chimes in Brian.

"Oh, don't worry," replies our guide, his eyes gleaming. "In another mile or so we'll be entering a twelve-mile-long gorge. That's where the action begins."

Our guide, Steve, is a tall, lean man in his mid fifties—a retired industrial arts teacher. Perfect for the two rowdies sitting up front, I think to myself.

"Remember," he continues, "when we hit the white stuff I'm

really going to need your help steering the raft. Everyone has to follow my instructions or we can get into real trouble. We've had a lot of rain lately, and the river is running pretty high today."

Steve gives us a quick refresher course on the paddling directions. "There will be times when I will call for everyone to paddle forward, or everyone backward, and then other times when I'll need everyone on one side of the raft to paddle forward and everyone on the other side to do the opposite. And when I say paddle, I mean *paddle!*"

While the current is still reasonably calm, we rehearse the latter maneuver and the raft turns in a sweeping circle. Steve reverses the call and the raft swings around the opposite way.

Spring is just arriving this far north. The snow has all melted, but the trees along the riverbanks are just beginning to awaken. Their multihued buds and flowers give a muted autumn effect. A red-tailed hawk soaring overhead goes unnoticed by all except Steve, Lex, and me. Everyone else's eyes remain riveted on the river in anticipation of our plunge into the gorge.

None of the kids seems to notice the growing roar of the river, which has been getting louder by the minute.

"Okay, get ready, everybody!" Steve calls out. "As soon as we round that bend up ahead we will start dropping down into the gorge. Listen for my instructions and remember two things: Keep your hand over the handle of your paddle so that you don't knock anyone's teeth out, and keep your feet tucked under the seat in front of you. That will keep you in the raft."

We negotiate the bend, and there is the first set of rapids about two hundred yards ahead. Now I understand why it's called whitewater rafting. The tempest of water rushing over the rocks is sending white froth flying everywhere. We begin gaining speed very quickly. Rapids indeed.

"ALL FORWARD!" Steve shouts. No doubt he wants to make sure the two boys in the front have a ride they will remember.

Within moments we are sucked into the torrent. No need to paddle now, so Steve instructs us to rest and hang on tight. When we career over a submerged rock, the front of the raft bounces up abruptly, sending Brian and Tyrone flying out of their seats. Much to my relief both boys come back down inside the raft and not in the river. The kids are laughing hysterically and yelling at the top of their lungs.

Suddenly, a large boulder looms up ahead, directly in our path.

"LEFT BACKWARDS, RIGHT FORWARD!" Steve hollers.

I'm glad to see that in the heat of the moment everyone still knows right from left. With Steve urging us to paddle harder, the raft slowly veers to the left. We miss the boulder by less than a foot.

After several breathtaking minutes we find ourselves speeding out of the first set of rapids as swiftly as we slipped into it. Thankfully there are no empty seats in the raft. Steve congratulates us on a job well done, and then in his next breath cautions us against becoming too relaxed because there is an even steeper set yet to come.

As we glide along a flat, gentle straightaway, Brian catches sight of the other group's rafts.

"Let's catch up to them!" he exhorts Steve.

"All forward" is the call, and with all of us paddling madly, we begin closing in on the next raft. It is filled with boys, and when they realize what is happening, they, too, start paddling forward with all their might. Then all of a sudden they reverse direction. Their guide, who seems to have a glint in his eye as permanent as Steve's, reaches behind him, pulls out a small hand pump, and hands it to the boy in front of him. Now they become a fireboat, the pump sending long streams of frigid water cascading down on our heads. Steve produces a similar weapon so that we can return fire.

The battle is on. Before long, the two rafts have gravitated close enough for the combatants to splash each other with their paddles. In the midst of the mutual drenching, the other guide has deftly managed to steer the rear of his raft up against the front of ours, where Brian has been launching one good-natured taunt after another at our opponents. Suddenly the guide snatches Brian by the life vest and tries to yank him aboard his raft. Tyrone and the two girls in the second seat grab on to Brian's various appendages, but they are no match for the strength of this well-built athlete in his early twenties.

As soon as the capture is complete, the guide pushes our raft off with his paddle and instructs his crew to paddle forward. They race away with their trophy like victorious pirates, and there is little we can do to stop them.

The second set of rapids lives up to its promise. But we're seasoned paddlers by now, and Steve guides us through without mishap. Some of the kids had pushed to spend the magazine money on a day at a large amusement park. I don't imagine anyone at this point thinks that a roller coaster would have provided more excitement than this wild ride down the untamed upper Hudson.

As we enter a long, calm stretch, the rafts pull off to the side for a rest stop. The guides produce waterproof sacks filled with snacks and thermoses full of hot, sweet tea. Everyone is famished, and the food disappears quickly. Most of the group gets out of the rafts to stretch their legs, but his captor tells Brian that he is still a prisoner and must stay put. The guide remains in his seat, ostensibly standing guard. But while he is munching a handful of trail mix and chatting with one of the other guides, he fails to notice that Brian has slowly stood up and taken a step toward the rear of the raft. By the time the guide realizes what is happening, it is already too late. Brian has leapt headfirst and is aiming straight for the guide's chest. The force of the impact sends the guide spilling over the edge of the raft and into the river.

Brian scampers to the shore, grinning wildly, his arms raised over his head in victory. He rejoins his classmates, most of whom witnessed his bold escape, and receives high-fives from everyone. Word quickly spreads among the rest of the guides, and they gather round to tease their fallen comrade for allowing a scrawny thirteen-year-old to get the best of him.

The day ends with a barbecue feast back at the equipment shed. The two young women doing the cooking are hard pressed to keep up with the appetites of fifty ravenous teenagers plus their guides and chaperones. When the first steaks come out tough and leathery—I suspect that the woman at the grill is a vegetarian—Tyrone and Brian start working their charm on her. She agrees to let them take over. The subsequent offerings come out tender and juicy, earning the boys much praise from the crowd.

It's been a good day for Brian. By the end of our adventure, he looks as calm as I have ever seen him.

While we were gone on our trip, Carl managed to break one of the basement windows of a house across the street from the school. He and Larry were out front right after three o'clock having a catch with a baseball, and one of Carl's tosses sailed long. Jeff successfully resisted the urge to yell at the boys for playing ball where they know they weren't supposed to and instead offered to help Carl fix the window. This isn't Carl's first broken pane. Never, however, has it been intentional. It's just that his reckless style of play makes him and window glass natural enemies. We don't punish kids for window breaking; rather we expect them to help repair and pay for the damage. In this instance Jeff has told Carl he will loan him the money and then find him some odd jobs around the school that he can do to earn the money to pay Jeff back.

After the accident, the first step is for Carl to ring the doorbell of the house and confess his crime. Ironically, the building belongs to three Italian women in their eighties who all attended school in our building when it housed the parish parochial school. Mary, who lives on the first floor of the four-story flat, answers the door. She is the youngest sister and often sits out on her stoop on sunny days, keeping watch over the neighborhood. While she doesn't know Carl by name, she immediately recognizes him when she opens the door.

Carl is respectful and apologetic and promises that he will fix the window first thing in the morning. Mary smiles back at Carl and thanks him for coming to tell her.

"I know a lot of boys would have run away," she said. "But you're a good boy, aren't you?"

Jeff, who knows Mary well, asks her if she will let them into the basement so that they can clean up the broken glass and put in a temporary pane of cardboard. When they are done, he gives Carl a ride home.

The next morning Carl and Jeff set out on the window project right after breakfast. The repair will take several hours because first they have to remove the bars from the window frame and then replace them after they have finished glazing the window. Carl does the measuring—he's an old pro at this point—and Jeff double-checks his accuracy. Because it's a single, large pane, it will be an expensive mistake if the glass they buy doesn't fit. Then the two head off to the hardware store in Jeff's car to buy the pane.

Carl and Jeff complete the window repair just in time for lunch. Mary shows teacher and student her gratitude by sending them back to school with a plate of sweet Italian cookies for dessert.

Back at school, Lex's class is basking in the afterglow of yesterday's adventure. Brian makes the rounds of the building recounting his glorious revenge against his kidnapper and then meets up with Dan so that they can put the finishing touches on their drums.

With three coats of varnish, the shining, honey-colored drum bodies are ready for the final step, lacing down the drumskins with strips of sinew that Dan and Brian have cut from the excess deer hide. Dan shows Brian how to take the awl and make holes around the edge of the skin for the sinew to pass through. Stretching the skin onto the wood is delicate work, because great care has to be taken not to tear it.

The slow, painstaking process is yet another challenge for Brian, but with Dan's reassurance and assistance, Brian does a magnificent job. When Brian shows up at school at the end of the day with the finished product, he is, very appropriately, bursting with pride.

Brian's problem in his previous school wasn't some sort of "behavioral disorder"; it was the passive nature of the curriculum that he was forced to ingest every day. Highly energetic kids need a learning environment that is as active as they are. They need work that has inherent meaning and adults that inspire— not coerce—them to do it.

Here I am reminded of Thomas Armstrong's take on ADHD in *The Myth of the ADD Child*. Armstrong writes that what so-called ADHD kids are actually suffering from is a deficit of stimulation and excitement.[1] At home, their lives are increasingly dominated by audio and visual media that encourage them to lead indoor lives and to substitute virtual for real experience. In school, the fears about standards have reduced the day to covering the material that will be on the high-stakes tests at the end of the year.

To compensate for the lack of engagement at home or in school, Armstrong suggests, certain children develop overly active nervous systems that replace internal stimuli with those that would normally come from the external world. When you put these same kids in an interesting, energetic environment, the "symptoms" suddenly disappear.

This echoes a similar observation made a generation earlier by Charles Silberman in *Crisis in the Classroom*, a now classic book written at the onset of the institutionalization of labeling and drugging children: "There seem not to be any disruptive youngsters, or even restless youngsters in informal classrooms," wrote Silberman, to which he later added, "It is not the children who are disruptive, it is the formal classroom that is disruptive—of childhood itself."[2]

12

Everywhere there are signs that the school year is winding down. Most days the building is virtually deserted as everyone takes advantage of the beautiful weather and scatters outdoors. There are so many options within walking distance—parks, ball fields, basketball courts, the Hudson River, and numerous museums and historical sites. And then there are the 250 acres of mostly wilderness land the school owns, where the kids can get lost in nature for the day, or overnight as well, and which is only forty minutes away by school van.

The last major in-school activity is preparing for the end-of-the-year talent show, which usually runs for ninety minutes or more. Already more than a dozen individuals or groups have signed up to perform, and there is always a flurry of last-minute ideas.

For the last few days, Walter, renowned for his deadpan humor, has been busy downloading dumb food jokes from the Internet. He's doing a pretty good job of keeping them secret, but I have managed to pry one loose from him: How do you make a hamburger roll? Take a hamburger to a hill and push it down.

Brian has two acts he's working on, one an ensemble and one a solo. For the former he has roped his classmates into a skit in which half the kids kneel on a couch with their legs tucked underneath them and shoes stuffed onto their kneecaps, so that they look like midgets. The other half stand behind them, hidden by a big blanket, with their arms reaching around the kids on the couch. The illusion is that these arms are the midgets' long arms, which then proceed to perform various grooming tasks such as nose blowing and hair and teeth brushing. It's a hilarious sight gag, with copious amounts of toothpaste always winding up in places it doesn't belong. For his solo performance, Brian has worked out a clever mime routine that closes with his pretending to descend a set of stairs. He does it behind an overturned folding table so that he actually disappears from sight—an ingenious effect he made up himself.

Upstairs, the preschool is working on a rendition of the venerable folk tale "Caps for Sale." One of the moms has cleverly turned plastic headbands into monkey ears and made long furry tails for the kids to tuck into their pants. And I have loaned the group my extensive collection of baseball caps. In the skit, the cap peddler goes about the village crying out, "Caps for sale! Caps for sale! Fifty cents a cap!" The peddler is played by Bhawin, a new young preschool teacher, who, with his olive complexion and bushy black mustache, bears a striking resemblance to the character in the book.

The jungle gym, with its long horizontal ladder, serves as a perfect tree for the monkeys to hide in with their stolen caps. Quite fittingly, it is Tanya—the alpha female of the five-year-olds—who has won the role of the monkey that sneaks up on the napping peddler, steals his caps, and then hands them up to the other monkeys. The play has its rough edges, but the beauty of theater with small children is that no matter what happens, their cuteness always carries the day.

Damian and Andrew have wrapped up the writing of Damian's play, which Damian has decided to name "The Dark Lord." It's an understatement to call it an extravaganza. He has enlisted almost every student in the first through sixth grades for the cast. Rehearsals have already begun, but they aren't going smoothly. Damian has confused being a director with being a dictator. On any given day he manages to alienate at least half of the actors. Defections are mounting.

When the show is on the verge of total collapse, Nancy offers Damian her services so that he can concentrate on his role as dark lord. He wisely accepts, and under her patient guidance, relative peace returns to the stage. All the kids who had quit in protest rejoin the cast and work feverishly to complete costumes and props. Damian finishes painting the various castle and battlefield backdrops, a task that keeps him wonderfully occupied as the year races fitfully to a close.

As the final days of school approach, Irene isn't declaring one way or the other whether William will return next year. My intuition tells me he won't. Recently William, his mom, and his new little brother have moved. I suspect that one of the primary reasons for their uptown move is to relocate into a neighborhood with one of the better public schools.

We neither see nor hear from Irene much. Her job allowed her only a month of maternity leave, and she has already placed the new baby in day care and returned to work. Lately she has been dropping William off in front of the school each morning instead of coming in like she used to, and then not picking him up until the conclusion of our after-school program at five-thirty. Nancy has phoned her several times to ask about William's status but always gets an answering machine and no return call.

When we ask William about next year, he looks embarrassed, mumbling the equivalent of "I don't know; my mother says she's still thinking about it."

Nancy and I talk the situation over and agree that Irene's recent lack of contact is probably a sign of her ambivalence. We know how much she values the school because she has expressed her gratitude on more than one occasion for the remarkable turnaround in her son's overall attitude. We also know that, for her, William's reading is a non-negotiable issue, and that we are not in a position to make any guarantees regarding when he will learn to do it. We wish it were different; however, granting William the freedom to choose what and when to learn has been an essential part of his learning to take responsibility for his actions.

Whatever Irene's decision, William is not the same child she half dragged over to the breakfast table in September. As I predicted then, he has done a good deal of his learning on the run this year. Unfortunately, a lot of that learning has not had so much to do with the straight-line acquisition of academic skills as it has with strengthening the foundation of his emotional, intellectual, and physical development.

William has begun to learn how to go after what he wants in life. He knows now that this doesn't mean getting everything immediately, that patience and persistence are involved. He has taken the initial steps toward setting limits on his behavior. Along the way, too, he has discovered that all adults are not his enemies. Perhaps most important, he has come to recognize the value of cooperative endeavor and has gained at least an inkling of how to engage in it. While he will probably always be a bit willful, his basic temperament no longer has the same oppositional edge. Besides, likely as not, he is going to need a strong will if he is going to navigate his way into adulthood successfully.

Should this turn out to be William's only year with us, hopefully he has acquired enough self-respect, self-confidence, and self-discipline to enable him to meet the demands of a conventional classroom—without drugs. The same boy who was about to start down the Ritalin road, had not his mother and father stumbled upon the Free School, has proven that he doesn't need his biochemistry artificially altered in order to control his impulses. We were indeed able to trust him with the run of the building, and when he switched onto the wrong track, he showed us a willingness to head back toward the right one.

Instead of Ritalin, what we have given William is a heavy dose of autonomy, self-regulation, and community. These aren't miracle cures by any means. But they are the best antidotes we have found to a society that is mass-producing hyperstimulated, unbonded children, kids it then proceeds to mass-regulate by chemical means.

Rather than get rid of William like his previous school did, we helped him to begin ridding himself of some of his self-defeating and antisocial strategies, so that he could gradually become a functional and valued member of the community. We recognized him for the unique individual that he is, and for his special gifts and talents. We neither rated him against other children nor insisted that he match up with a set of contrived developmental standards. Whenever his behavior strayed too far from acceptable limits, we—students as well as teachers— established the kinds of natural consequences that would steer him toward choosing to act differently the next time. We refused to coerce him into a submissive docility that so often only serves to mask smoldering fires of failure, rage, and disaffection—and turns children into human time bombs.

And then, so suddenly it seems, the last day of school arrives. Nancy and I get together during breakfast to discuss details of the day and can only shrug our shoulders in wonder. Where has the year gone? It always blows by so fast.

We're blessed with a beautifully crisp summer day, thankfully not too hot. The upstairs big room, where this afternoon's festivities will be held, can be stifling when the outside temperature approaches ninety, fortunately an uncommon occurrence until the height of summer in these northern latitudes.

The atmosphere inside the school is a blend of sadness and excitement. We become so deeply attached to one another each year that leaving is never easy, for both those who are departing and even for those who are remaining behind. But the sense of loss is tempered by the anticipation of this afternoon's show and the long summer days ahead. For the four graduating girls in Lex's class, all of whom have been in the school for many years, there is an eagerness to leave the nest and land in a larger environment where there will be more young people their age and more opportunities to explore the world around them.

For the other two eighth graders, Brian and Tyrone, there is an anxious wondering: Will it be different this time in a system that seemed to have no place for them before?

William comes in looking very pensive, not at all his usual animated self. He tells us that his mother still hasn't decided about next year, and, further, that his mother won't be able to come to the show because she has to work.

Nancy and I have already decided that, in the absence of any official word from Irene, we will give William a proper farewell just in case. Nancy has bought a Native American medicine pouch for him to put special things in. To start him off, she has already placed in it a few precious stones for guidance and protection. We have also prepared for him the traditional gift that every departing Free Schooler receives: a large white T-shirt on which everyone has drawn or written a special message and signed in permanent Magic Marker. Each shirt becomes a multicolored memento unique from any other.

The school is a bit frenzied and chaotic, with everyone caught up in last-minute preparations for the graduation ceremony and talent show. But it is peaceful at the same time. Rarely are there ever any council meetings on the last day. A full dress rehearsal of the show, with the preschoolers for an audience, occupies the second half of the morning and takes us right up to lunchtime.

After lunch, teachers and interns who aren't busy helping kids get ready for the show convert the upstairs big room into a makeshift auditorium. This time the jungle gym is left in position. It will serve as a prop in the little kids' play and as the place where the preschoolers can perform aerial stunts. The altar, the last remaining vestige of the building's first incarnation as a nineteenth-century immigrant church, will serve as the backdrop for the main stage.

At one o'clock the room starts filling up with parents, grandparents, neighbors, and other assorted guests. One of the graduating girls volunteered an afternoon a week for the entire year at a day-care center for the infants of young mothers trying to finish high school: the nun who runs it and one of her staff are here. So is Brian's mentor, Dan. Soon it will be standing room only.

Betsy arrives with several large vases full of flowers, some that she has gleaned from neighborhood gardens and some that she purchased from a downtown flower shop. She rapidly arranges them into small bouquets that will be used to acknowledge all the volunteers that have supported the school over the course of the year, herself included.

By one-thirty all of the necessary guests have arrived. Another graduating girl's mother, who is an ordained minister, opens the ceremony with a nondenominational blessing. I welcome everyone and thank all for coming, and Nancy gives a brief reflection on the school year. Then, one by one, the teachers call up their students and present them with an award. These aren't competitive honors such as "Best Student." Rather, each is a sort of talisman, an acknowledgment of something special about a particular child. Our awards have titles such as the "Courage Award" or the "Albert Einstein Critical Thinker's Award." We spend an hour or more at the final teachers' meeting conferring until we come up with just the right award for every student.

Now it's time to say good-bye to the nongraduates who are leaving. Tanya comes to the stage beaming. Missy unveils Tanya's Free School T-shirt for the audience to see, and helps her put it on over her pretty summer dress. Then Missy gives Tanya her farewell gift, a large sketchpad and a set of colored markers, and then a big hug.

When Nancy calls William's name, he only reluctantly leaves his seat, and Nancy has to coax him onto the stage. He leans against her sheepishly while she tells him what a great year he has had and how much we will miss him if he doesn't return in September. I am reminded of his first day, when he clung so persistently to his mother's side. This year he has truly come full circle.

We always save the graduates for last. When Lex calls Brian's name, Brian charges forward, his arms raised in victory just as they were that day on the river. I don't think he could smile any wider if he tried. His little preschool buddies all yell out his name, and there are affectionate catcalls from his classmates. The audience quiets while Lex reads Brian the inscription on his diploma, but pandemonium breaks out again when Brian dons his Free School T-shirt and raises his arms back over his head. Somehow I don't think we've seen the last of him.

After a brief intermission while the performers get themselves organized, it's showtime. Walter comes out first to warm up the crowd with a dozen or so of his jokes, each one worse than the previous one. His expressionless delivery is perfect, and the audience groans.

The preschoolers' play brings down the house, just as I expected it would. Tanya is the epitome of giggly slyness as she sneaks up on the unsuspecting peddler, removes the stack of caps from his snoring head, and distributes them among her fellow monkeys. The only hitch comes when three-year-old Marcus forgets to hold on to the jungle gym while he is trying to fit a cap over his monkey ears and slips and falls. He lands butt-first with a dull *thunk* on the padded rug below. Thankfully, his mother, seated nearby, is able to scoop him up before he starts to cry.

There are a few little kid aerial acts while the audience is still facing the jungle gym, and then the seventh and eighth graders haul a couch out onto the main stage for their midget act. They really ham it up this time. Hair gets brushed in the wrong direction and toothpaste finds its way into ears and noses. The audience laughs hysterically, especially the preschoolers, who are seated in little chairs in the front two rows.

Brian remains on the stage after the couch is carried off and performs his mime routine with a smooth confidence. The audience oohs and aahs when he descends the imaginary stairs and disappears from sight.

Damian's play, which runs for nearly twenty minutes, is the last act on this year's program and makes for a very fit ending. The plot involves a titanic contest between good and evil. Three demon lords, led by Damian, dressed in a black, hooded robe and carrying a very long sword, are attempting to conquer the world and place it forever under their dominion. They are within moments of victory in the final scene when an army of angels led by the angel queen, played by Tiffany, descends from their heavenly castle to battle the demon lords. The stage fills up with dead and wounded, until the queen and the dark lord are the only two characters left standing. After a furious struggle, Tiffany, in real life an adept student of the martial arts, cleverly wrests the dark lord's sword away from him and turns it on him to strike a mortal blow. The dark lord swoons, and the audience erupts into a standing ovation.

Just what have we accomplished with Damian this year? Nothing tangible, certainly; nothing that can be measured in test scores or grade point averages. What we have done is to help free a troubled ten-year-old boy from the drug-induced bondage in which his mother found him in November, and allow that which was being chemically suppressed to begin to express and untangle itself. Rather than force Damian to conform to some modern, sanitized version of boyhood, we have given him the space to be his own quirky, highly imaginative self, to make mistakes and then learn from them.

Along the way, what Damian has discovered is that there are appropriate, self-enhancing ways to be the center of attention. His leadership style, as we have seen, needs work. For this reason I'm glad he'll be returning next year, so that he will have many more opportunities to learn how to lead effectively, as well as how to interact happily with other children as a peer, or even as a follower. He has a long way to go in that department, too.

Damian, most important, has demonstrated that it isn't necessary to drug him in order for him to manage his behavior. He has made real strides this year toward learning to govern his impulses and to modulate his energy and emotions. While he remains in many ways a frightened, angry child—and for good reason—a more at ease Damian is beginning to emerge. I remain convinced that this change never would have been possible were he still being kept in the thrall of the biopsychiatric drugs he had been forced to take since the age of five.

We, too, wish that Paula had found us sooner. By the time she brought her son to us, he had already spent half his lifetime within a stigmatizing school structure where the name of the game was to deaden, if not outright eliminate, his distress signals, to deindividualize, if not dehumanize, him. Through no fault of his overwhelmed, routine-bound teachers I am sure, little heed was given to the question of why Damian was so anxious, so flighty, and, when cornered, so hostile and defiant. They never asked him to draw a portrait of himself so that they could see for themselves the deep fissure that runs through the middle of his psyche—a split that only coldly cynical men and women of science would say was caused by faulty genes. To all those experts who claim that Damian's state of being is biologically predetermined, I pose the following question: How intimately do you get to know the stories of the children—and their families—before you so readily recommend that they be labeled and drugged?

The effect of those five years Damian spent as a "problem child" in conventional classrooms was to reinforce, not relieve, the dysfunctional patterns of thought, emotion, and action that Damian developed in response to the confused and traumatic conditions of his early childhood. Let us remember, too, that a significant part of Damian's "problem" in his earlier school experience was his willful, individualistic nature. Those environments, based on conformity and blind obedience, continually demanded that he betray himself.

The same can be said for the others whose adventures I have chronicled in this book. They have all encountered obstacles to the natural unfolding of their development, some more than others. What all of them have needed is not more external control, biochemical or otherwise, but rather the opportunity to participate in that unfolding—to be active agents of their own education, not passive recipients of skills and knowledge.

And they have needed, even more than patient teaching and loving guidance, the freedom to be themselves.

Conclusion

It is not a beautiful day in the neighborhood when millions of American boys in their prime developmental years—our society's future men—are being forced to participate in a drug experiment of staggering proportions. It is equally unacceptable that as many as a million of our future women have already been assigned the same fate. Not only are we ignorant of the long-term effects of biopsychiatric drugs on children, but we also lack any real evidence that they are in fact aiding children's development. Yet their use only continues to spread.

Even the National Institutes of Health (NIH), upon whom the federal government relies for the data to underpin national education and mental health policies, grudgingly concedes that there remains no sound scientific basis for the labeling and drugging of children. In November 1998, NIH held a Consensus Development Conference on ADHD and its treatment in order to clear away once and for all the doubt and ambiguity that have continued to cloud the issue. Consensus conferences are convened in order for experts to present scientific data about controversial treatments to an independent jury, which, after hearing all of the evidence, writes a final consensus statement. The statement is then handed out to the press and posted on the NIH web site.[1]

Since, historically, NIH-funded research has overwhelmingly supported labeling and drugging, and the presenting experts were all selected by Dr. Peter Jensen, an increasingly staunch defender of biopsychiatric approaches to dealing with nonconforming children, the conclusions reached by the jury are surprising indeed. There were a number of startling admissions embedded in the text of the consensus statement, buried amid the usual ADHD language. For instance, after raising fundamental questions about whether ADHD is a "valid diagnosis," the authors also admitted the failure of researchers to produce enough data to indicate that ADHD is due to brain malfunction.

Then the authors wrote quite succinctly about the most relevant issue of all, the efficacy of the biopsychiatric "treatment" of children: "Of concern are the consistent findings that despite the improvement in core symptoms, there is little improvement in academic achievement or social skills."[2]

The document did not specify what is meant by "core symptoms," but one can safely assume the authors were referring to the myriad behavioral traits that exasperate so many parents and teachers: inattentiveness, restlessness, impulsivity, rebelliousness, and aggressiveness. In other words, the independent jury—whose independence was questionable at best—reached the same conclusion that I have come to in my work, namely that labeling and drugging ultimately serve one, and only one, purpose: the control of disruptive children.

The statement ended with a deadening thud: "Finally, after years of clinical research and experience with ADHD, our knowledge about the cause or causes of ADHD remains speculative. Consequently, we have no strategies for the prevention of ADHD."[3]

Thus, the assembled experts from across the land were still asking parents and teachers to take it on faith that a neurological disease with no known causes and no strategies for its prevention is running rampant through our youth population. On such a slim evidentiary basis more and more defenseless children are being diagnosed and drugged every day. What could be more mythological?

It is imperative that we not give in to the seductive quick fix of attaching biological names to children's distress signals and then giving the children pills to suppress those signals. As parents, teachers, and other professionals that work with young people, we must stand our ground and look more deeply for ways to help kids grow up happy and whole.

My goal has been to present an alternative vision. By letting you in on the day-to-day school lives of a handful of distressed children, I hoped to demonstrate that it is absolutely unnecessary to alter children's biochemistry in order for them to control themselves and become successful learners. I have tried to show that William, Damian, Carl, Brian, Walter, Mark, Mumasatou, Gaby, Tanya, and the millions of others like them don't have a disorder. And they don't need medication, because they're not sick.

What these children do need is a society that is less toxic to their development, that supports their families, that honors their individuality and uniqueness. They need schools that educate according to how the brain actually learns, rather than to some outmoded Skinnerian dogma. They need teachers who are loving guides and role models, not rigid taskmasters. They need psychological support systems that respond to them with insight and compassion instead of pathological labels and biopsychiatric drugs. Above all, they need the fundamental acceptance of who they are, not a medicalized critique of where they aren't on some standardized developmental scale.

To reduce the story of a distressed child to a tale of misbegotten biochemistry is a terrible thing. It's the approach of snake oil salesmen, another step toward the capture of children by an economy that views them only as present and future consumers.

My highest aim in writing this book was to show that every child has a unique story, one that is comprised of many different elements: inborn temperament; gender, race, and social class; parental attitudes and beliefs; childcare providers and schools; and the surrounding culture. In cases in which children are in fact distressed and not just reacting to an environment that is too restrictive or insensitive to their needs, the causes of the distress cannot be found in any single element. They can be found only in the entirety of children's stories, where the signs pointing to what is wrong or missing are encrypted in their scripts like images in a dream.

Perhaps this is the reason why the NIH consensus panel was forced to admit the failure of the experts to locate either the causes of the conglomeration of behavioral traits they have labeled ADHD or any effective ways to prevent them: They were looking for something that doesn't exist, and even if it did, they were looking in the wrong place.

To solve any problem, it must first be correctly identified and defined. In the case of distressed children, once the signals contained in a child's behavior are successfully interpreted, it becomes possible both to create effective solutions to existing problems and to prevent the onset of future ones. For instance, if one of the troubles is a substance-abusing parent, then he or she can be encouraged, or mandated, if necessary, to get help. If another is marital discord, then the parents can seek out couples counseling. If a child is suffering from lack of attention from one or both parents, they can be urged to spend more time with their son or daughter. If excessive television viewing is one of the culprits, then the amount of time spent watching TV can be reduced and other activities put in its place. If the school environment is not responsive to a child's individual needs, then the parents can request that the classroom regimen be adapted to fit their child, or they can remove the child from the situation altogether.

Science strenuously avoids examining these emotional and psychosocial dimensions of human existence because they are, as Robert Coles writes in the preface to the new edition of *The Mind's Fate: A Psychiatrist Looks at His Profession*, "so messy and unpredictable."⁴ They are filled with endless shades of gray and very little black or white. They don't lend themselves to tidy computer models or sweeping social policies.

The fact of the matter is that helping to repair children's emotional or cognitive structures is not simple. Change that doesn't come in a pill is gradual. It progresses in fits and starts and takes time. Moreover, certain elements of the problem can prove to be intractable. Economic pressures may make it difficult if not impossible for a parent, or parents, to give their kids the attention for which they are crying out. An abusive parent may choose to remain in denial, or an unhappy couple may refuse to get help. Parents who are unable to convince teachers and administrators that the classroom environment is the problem, not their child, may feel they have no other educational options. Likewise, many teachers are reluctant to loosen the reins and experiment with more creative approaches to teaching. They fear losing control of the classroom and, worse still, their jobs. The increasing standardization of the curriculum and reliance on high stakes testing leaves teachers no choice but to forego improvisation and stick to the lesson plan.

Unfortunately, there are no magic bullets. At the Free School we can by no means claim a 100 percent success rate with kids like Damian and William. We have been able to help a great many children and families, but not all of them. However, I have yet to encounter a student who I thought would genuinely benefit from biopsychiatric drugs.

There are important postscripts to some of the kids' stories. We continued to see Tanya even after she left our school because her little brother remained in our preschool and she would accompany her mother when Marta dropped Beejay off every other Monday morning after he spent the weekend with them. Tanya had no trouble whatsoever adjusting to public school life. She was doing very well academically, and Marta wasn't getting any negative feedback about Tanya's behavior. Tanya reported gleefully that she liked her teacher and her teacher liked her.

Brian's transition wasn't nearly as smooth. Initially, he and his mother opted against his returning to the same suburban school district from whence he had come to us. Instead he tried a small Christian high school that is renowned for its high-level basketball program. The only problem was that he never made it to basketball season. The school had rigid rules and a conservative academic structure, neither of which suited a free spirit like Brian. Moreover, he was one of only two Caucasian kids in the entire school. It was a bad fit in every way, and Brian was gone before Thanksgiving.

Brian then declared himself ready for his local public school, but he really wasn't. He immediately fell into bad behavioral and academic habits that persisted for some months. Much to his credit, however, he stuck it out, and by the end of the school year we heard reports that he was beginning to settle down and succeed. Then the following summer Brian and his mother moved to Vermont, where he successfully completed an employment training program and earned his G.E.D.

Damian, who was supposed to return to us the following September, ended up going back to live with his father just before school started. By the end of the summer, apparently, Damian had reverted to his old defiant ways, and Paula felt she could no longer handle parenting him as well as a new baby.

Damian's dad enrolled him in the local public school, where things went badly from the start. I soon received a long-distance call from Damian's new teacher. A seasoned veteran, she nonetheless was fast growing weary of Damian's disruptiveness and frequent refusals to do the assigned work. I described at length the ways in which we had worked with him, adding that if he had been unwillingly sent to his father's—as I very much suspected—then her task was probably a thankless one. I suggested that she give Damian as much responsibility and freedom of movement as possible. One-on-one contact with a teacher, preferably male, would be advisable, too.

This sensible, experienced teacher, already well versed in dealing with difficult boys like Damian, agreed implicitly with everything I was saying. However, she was severely limited in her options. There were twenty-five other children in the room, and her small-town school had few adjunct resources. Unable to offer her much reassurance, I thanked her for caring enough about Damian to take the time to call and sincerely wished her good luck. I could tell she wasn't someone who gave up easily.

The next thing we knew, Damian was at our door. He had begged his mother to let him come home, promising to behave better, and she finally relented. What made the real difference, I think, was the fact that Damian's dad had told Paula the school was urging him to put Damian back on Ritalin, a road she did not want to see her son go down again.

We were chagrined—but certainly not surprised given what he had just been through—to discover that Damian had regressed considerably. Slowly, fitfully, he began to resettle, and then, as suddenly as he had reappeared, he announced that he wanted to transfer to the public school in his neighborhood across the river from Albany. He said he had met a girl who went there and that he wanted to go to school with her.

Paula refused even to entertain the idea of Damian's switching schools. She told him they were certain to insist that he resume taking drugs. Given his most recent experience, I had a hard time finding fault with her logic.

But Damian didn't. He pestered his mother incessantly at home to let him go, and in school his behavior deteriorated badly. He even began stealing, something he had never done the year before. Each time he was caught in another delinquent act his explanation was the same: "I don't want to be here anymore. I want to go to the school near my house."

In one such conversation, when I reminded him how poorly things had just gone in the public school up north, he shot back, eyes glaring with determination, "I can do the work; it's easy. And this time I'll listen to the teacher."

There was clearly no future in holding Damian hostage. When he continued to escalate his appeals, we called Paula in for a conference in order to tell her that we couldn't go on keeping Damian against his will. It just wasn't working. At this point he was bound and determined to get us to expel him, an outcome that would only damage his self-esteem even more. I urged her to take Damian at his word, citing numerous examples from the past in which kids like Damian, who were hellbent on returning to public school, had, in fact, made successful transitions.

Paula remained unconvinced. She was very afraid that her son would be relabeled and drugged. Moreover, she was adamant that Damian not get his way this time. I tried repeatedly to help her to see the situation in a different light, saying that it wasn't the same as a power struggle over bedtimes or TV watching or household chores. She finally accepted, albeit grudgingly, that it was no longer a viable option for Damian to remain in the Free School. But he was not going back to public school—period, end of discussion.

Nancy and I suggested that Paula take the rest of the week to think things over. On Monday she came in with Damian and informed us that she had made arrangements with her sister and her father to help her homeschool Damian for the rest of the school year.

That would be the last we would hear from Paula until the following July, when she telephoned me to say that she had finally decided to respect Damian's wishes and allow him to enroll in a voluntary summer academic program at their neighborhood school. He was getting all A's and B's, she reported elatedly, and was slated to join a regular sixth grade class in the fall. She thanked me profusely for all we had done for them, and ended by sharing that now she could see the importance of allowing children to make their own choices, live them out, and then learn from their experience.

I thanked her in return for making my day with such excellent news.

Meanwhile, William didn't come back in September, either. Just as we thought she might, Irene enrolled him in the public school near their new uptown apartment, where he was placed in a regular second grade classroom. Then, one evening in late October, Nancy's phone rang and it was none other than young William himself. He said he wanted her to know that he was doing okay in his new school. Better still, he went on, he was learning to read and loving every minute of it. He said he missed the Free School a lot, but that he liked his teacher and had made several friends. He promised to come back to visit us the first chance he got.

William called me right after he finished speaking with Nancy. He gave me more or less the same report, adding that he found learning to read pretty easy. Then we reminisced for a while. He asked about each of the kids who had been in his class last year and wondered especially how his furry pal Lakota was doing. I marveled to myself at how articulate and mature William sounded.

When William was all talked out, Irene got on the line and began thanking me over and over for helping her son. She considered it nothing short of a miracle that he was functioning so successfully in a regular classroom without Ritalin.

Later in the conversation Irene confided that she and her husband had separated permanently, but that William Senior was continuing to help support them financially and talked with the boys regularly by telephone. Then she apologized for not being more forthright about her intention to shift William Junior back to a conventional school. I replied that she had absolutely no reason to be sorry. She had been struggling through a very difficult period and was absolutely right to concentrate on taking care of herself and her family. Besides, I continued, she more than anyone knew what was best for her son. And who could argue with her choice? William was happy, doing well in school, and learning to read with ease.

I don't remember Irene ever sounding so relaxed.

Happily, the public perception of the labeling and drugging of children has begun to shift since I began writing this book. At that time there appeared to be little awareness of the extent of society's reliance on biopsychiatric drugs to manage children's behavior. Today, however, expressions of concern and opposition are beginning to appear all across the country. Class-action lawsuits have been filed in federal courts in Texas, California, and New Jersey, claiming that Ritalin manufacturer Novartis and the American Psychiatric Association conspired to create a market for Ritalin and expand its use. State legislatures in a growing number of states are passing legislation to prevent schools from recommending or requiring that parents put their children on biopsychiatric drugs. Minnesota became the first to bar schools and child protection agencies from ordering parents to drug their kids, and next Connecticut went a step further by prohibiting any school staff member from discussing drug treatments with a parent. Similar bills have been introduced in a dozen other states. The legislative push is a reaction to what its advocates call overprescription of the drugs. They argue that an excessive reliance on Ritalin and several competing drugs is driving parents away from traditional forms of discipline and is creating a growing illicit traffic in these potent and dangerous drugs.

All the while the debate grows more polarized. There's little wonder that so much controversy exists. It is a very sensitive and complex matter involving the lives of millions of individual children, their developmental processes, their psychological dynamics, and their interactions with the surrounding culture. It involves the parents, their parenting styles, their educational beliefs, their reactions to having difficult children, and the dynamics of the family. It involves the schools, which is where, we must remember, the impetus to classify and label children began in the first place. Our system of public education in this country has been in a state of crisis for decades. It is constantly grasping at straws—and searching for scapegoats. It also involves the medical system, with its increasing tendency to view the mind and body as machines, to see all imbalances as purely biochemical in origin, and then to respond, in turn, with potent biochemical agents.

And, lest we forget, extremely influential economic interests are at work in this issue as well. The pharmaceutical manufacturers are some of the most powerful corporations in the world, and profits from the sale of biopsychiatric drugs are soaring. The brave new world of managed health care favors their use because they are "cost effective." Moreover, school districts, and now certain parents, receive government funding for labeled children. Diagnoses such as ADHD, in other words, trigger the flow of substantial sums of money through the American economy.

I have made little attempt to tell both sides of the ADHD story. Rather, I tried to make my bias clear from the start. It is a bias based not only on theory, but also on nearly thirty years of experience with children and families of every imaginable type. Thus, I will say it one final time: To conclude that distressed children simply have faulty brain chemistry and to categorize millions of them as though they are in some way defective is to take the easy way out. It provides the basis for a thinly veiled Orwellian social policy that threatens the futures—and the very souls—of our nation's children.

Surely there is a better way.

Notes

Introduction

1. Peter Breggin, *Talking Back to Ritalin* (Cambridge: Perseus, 2001), 3.
2. Julie Zito et al., "Trends in the Prescription of Psychotropic Medications to Preschoolers," *Journal of the American Medical Association* 283, no. 8 (February 23, 2000): 1025–30.
3. Joseph Pearce, from a lecture given in Albany, New York, October 1992.

CHAPTER 2

1. George Dennison, *The Lives of Children* (New York: Random House, 1969), 22.
2. John Gatto, *Dumbing Us Down: The Hidden Curriculum of Compulsory Schooling* (Philadelphia: New Society Publishers, 1992), 29.
3. David Boadella, *Wilhelm Reich: His Life and Work* (New York: Arkana Books, 1972), 116.

CHAPTER 3

1. Robert Coles, *The Mind's Fate: A Psychiatrist Looks at His Profession* (Boston: Little, Brown, 1995), xvii–xx.
2. Paul MacLean, *The Triune Concept of the Brain and Behavior* (Toronto: University of Toronto Press, 1973), 7–9.
3. Chris Mercogliano and Kim Debus, "An Interview with Joseph Chilton Pearce," *Journal of Family Life* 5, no. 1, 20–21.

CHAPTER 4

1. James Hillman, *The Soul's Code* (New York: Random House, 1996), 6.

CHAPTER 5

1. Breggin, *Talking Back*, 51–53.
2. Ibid., 67–68.
3. Ibid., 85.
4. Ibid., 72.
5. Bruce Bower, untitled article in *Science News* 135 (June 18, 1988): 399.
6. Breggin, *Talking Back*, 111.
7. A.S. Neill, *Summerhill: A Radical Approach to Childrearing* (New York: Simon and Schuster, 1977), 4.

CHAPTER 6

1. Chris Mercogliano, *Making It Up As We Go Along* (Portsmouth, N.H.: Heinemann, 1998), 20–37.
2. Robert Bly, *Sibling Society* (New York: Addison-Wesley, 1996), 44.
3. James Garbarino, *Raising Children in a Socially Toxic Environment* (San Francisco: Jossey-Bass, 1995), 4.
4. Ibid., 153.
5. Joseph Biederman, "Family-Environment Risk Factors for ADHD," *Archives of General Psychiatry* 52 (June 1993): 464–70.
6. Ashley Montagu, *Touching: The Human Significance of the Skin* (New York: Columbia University Press, 1971), 190.
7. Marianna Caplin, *Untouched* (Prescott, Ariz.: Hohm Press, 1998), 6.

CHAPTER 7

1. Ronald Davis, *The Gift of Dyslexia* (New York: Berkley Publishing Group, 1997), 9.
2. Elizabeth Carlson, Deborah Jacobvitz, and Alan Sroufe, *Child Development* 58 (1987): 1488–95.
3. Paul Jensen et al., "Psychosocial and Medical Histories of Stimulant-Treated Children," *Journal of the American Academy of Child and Adolescent Psychiatry* 27, no. 6 (1988): 798–801.
4. John Bowlby, "Developmental Psychiatry Comes of Age," *American Journal of Psychiatry* 135, no. 1 (January 1988): 1–9.

CHAPTER 8

1. Cayley David, *Ivan Illich in Conversation* (Ontario: Anansi Press, 1992), 21.

2. Barbara Kantrowitz and Claudia Kalb, "How to Build a Better Boy." *Newsweek* CXXXI, no. 19 (May 11, 1998).

CHAPTER 9

1. Merrelyn Emery, "The Neurological Effects of Television Viewing on Children," (Ph.D. diss., Australian National University, Canberra, 1973).
2. Martin Pawley, *A Private Future* (New York: Random House, 1974), 128.
3. Dorothy Singer and Jerome Singer, "Television Viewing and Aggressive Behavior in Preschool Children: A Field Study," *Annals of Forensic Psychiatry* 347 (1980): 289–303.
4. Mercogliano and Debus, "An Interview," 23.
5. Keith Buzzell, from a letter to the author.

CHAPTER 10

1. Sylvia Ashton-Warner, *Teacher* (New York: Simon and Schuster, 1963), 33.
2. Joseph Pearce, *The Biology of Transcendence* (Rochester, N.Y.: Park St. Press, 2001), 104–5.
3. Alfie Kohn, *Punished by Rewards: The Trouble with Gold Stars, Incentive Plans, "A's," Praise and Other Bribes* (Boston: Houghton Mifflin, 1993), 52.

CHAPTER 11

1. Thomas Armstrong, *The Myth of the ADD Child* (New York: Penguin Putnam, 1995), 30.
2. Charles Silberman, *Crisis in the Classroom* (New York: Random House, 1964), 196.

Conclusion

1. The web site address for the Consensus Statement is http://consensus.nih.gov/cons/110/110_statement.pdf.
2. National Institutes of Health, "Diagnosis and Treatment of Attention Deficit Hyperactivity Disorder: NIH Consensus Statement" 16, no. 2 (November 16–18): 10.
3. Ibid., 3.
4. Coles, *The Mind's Fate*, xiv.

Recommended Reading

Armstrong, Thomas, *The Myth of the ADD Child*. Penguin Books, 1995.

Ashton-Warner, Sylvia, *Teacher*. Simon and Schuster, 1963.

Bly, Robert, *The Sibling Society*. Addison-Wesley, 1996.

Breeding, John, *The Wildest Colts Make the Best Horses*. Bright Books, 1996.

Breggin, Peter, *Talking Back to Ritalin*. Perseus Publishing, 2001.

Breggin, Peter and Ginger, *The War Against Children of Color*. Common Courage Press, 1998.

Buzzell, Keith, *The Children of Cyclops*. Wyllaned Books, 1998.

deGrandpre, Richard, *Ritalin Nation*. Norton, 1999.

Dennison, George, *Lives of Children*. Random House, 1969.

Foucault, Michel, *Madness and Civilization*. Random House, 1988.

Foucault, Michel, *Discipline and Punish*. Random House, 1995.

Garbarino, James, *Raising Children in a Socially Toxic Environment*. Jossey-Bass, 1995.

Gatto, John, *Dumbing Us Down*. New Society Publishers, 1992.

Gatto, John, *The Underground History of American Education*. Oxford Village Press, 2001.

Goertz, Donna, *Children Who Are Not Yet Peaceful*. North Atlantic Books, 2001.

Hart, Leslie, *On Learning and the Human Brain*. Brain Age Publishers, 1983.

Hartmann, Thom, *Complete Guide to ADHD*. Underwood Books, 2000.

Holt, John, *Freedom and Beyond*. Dell, 1972.

Holt, John, *How Children Fail*. Perseus Books, 1995.

Holt, John, *How Children Learn*. Perseus Books, 1995.

Illich, Ivan, *Deschooling Society*. Harper and Row, 1972.

Illich, Ivan, *Tools for Conviviality*. Harper, 1973.

Kohl, Herb, *I Won't Learn from You*. New Press, 1994.

Levine, Mel, *A Mind at a Time*. Simon and Schuster, 2002.

Pearce, Joseph Chilton, *Evolution's End*. Harper San Francisco, 1992.

Pearce, Joseph Chilton, *The Biology of Transcendence*. Park Street Press, 2001.

Pert, Candace, *Molecules of Emotion*. Simon and Schuster, 1999.

Acknowledgments

First and foremost, I want to honor the children at the Free School and their families, whose steadfast determination to be themselves inspired me to turn their stories into this teaching tale.

Special thanks also go to Fred Bay and the J. B. Paul and C. M. Paul Foundation, without whose support this book might never have seen the light of day; to my agent, Jill Grinberg, and my editor at Beacon Press, Joanne Wyckoff, for taking a chance on such an unusual project; and, finally, to my wife, Betsy, for putting up with all my ranting.